TABLE OF CONTENTS

THAILAND

Travel Guide 2017

Casey Knowls

1. Welcome to Thailand

Thailand is known around the world as 'The Land of Smiles'. But you probably already knew that. What's less clear is whether this really refers to the locals, or to the many millions of tourists who migrate there each year. Because this is a country that really has it all. It's a place to fall in love with. There's a reason why you don't meet many people who've only been to Thailand one time. You visit once, and you're hooked. It's addictive.

It's the second-most visited country in Asia. It's the fourteenth-most visited country in the entire world, ahead of big-hitters Greece, Canada, Japan. According to some surveys, Bangkok attracts more tourists than any other city on Earth.

So what is it about this place? What is it that attracted nearly 30 million visitors in 2015 (an enormous 20% rise on the previous year)? Why do people keep going back, and back, and back again?

In this chapter we're going to dig into Thailand as a whole, seeking to discover the unique recipe that's whipped up such a buffet of tourism. We'll be looking at the **geography** and **climate**; its **history** and **economy**. For a closer look at the Thai people themselves, bide your time until the next chapter.

Are you ready? Let's go.

Geography

It's true that Thailand's booming tourist industry is largely thanks to an incredible amount of work that's gone in to building foreigner-friendly travel infrastructure. But, you also have to say that it was dealt a good hand by Mother Nature. The geography can be summed up in two words: diverse, and spectacular.

For the purposes of this book, and for the sake of simplicity, we're later going to break the country down into three broad regions: the north, the middle and the south.

To help you get a nice, in-depth feel for the country's layout in this introduction, though, here's an overview of the generally-accepted six regions of Thailand.

1) Northern Thailand

Borders Myanmar and Laos, the three countries coming together to form the infamous Golden Triangle.

Home to historical hipster haven Chiang Mai, and the White Temple in Chiang Rai (if you've ever browsed a brochure about Thailand, or looked it up online in any way, you've seen the White Temple. It's pretty hard to miss.).

Big, green mountains abound, including Thailand's tallest, Doi Inthanon (2,565m, since you ask). There are lots, and lots, and lots of mountains. It's really quite beautiful.

2) Northeastern Thailand

Home to the enormous and arid Khorat Plateau... and not much else.

OK, so that's a little reductive – it's actually Thailand's most populated region, with approximately 20 million residents – but for our purposes we can quickly move on. It's unlikely you'll be visiting, unless you're passing through on your way to Laos.

3) Western Thailand

Most of Thailand's 2,100km-long border with Myanmar runs down the country's mountainous western flank, with vast forests and river valleys aplenty.

Kanchanaburi is the largest province in the region, home to Erawan National Park and, most famously, the bridge on the River Kwai (as seen in... what's that film called again? Oh, The Bridge on the River Kwai). Both are certainly worth visiting; both can be easily seen on a day trip from Bangkok.

4) Central Thailand

Known as 'The Rice Bowl of Asia', this tasty-sounding region is the agricultural heart of the country, with the Chao Phraya river providing fertile land for the area's phalanxes of farmers.

It's home to the country's former capital Ayutthaya, pleasant seaside town Hua Hin, and, of course, the little-known city of Bangkok.

5) Eastern Thailand

The smallest of Thailand's six regions, but still popular with tourists, it borders Cambodia to the east and the Gulf of Thailand to the west and south.

The region's biggest attraction is Pattaya. It's a seaside town that has a reputation for attracting – how can we say this? – a certain type of tourist. Male, getting on in years... you get the picture. That really doesn't give the city its due however; there's plenty more on offer.

Elsewhere the region has plenty more delights, including Thailand's first national park, Khao Yai, and a number of islands just off the coast which are a little less developed than their cousins across the Gulf.

Speaking of which...

6) Southern Thailand

Arguably the image that will most quickly come to a person's mind when they hear 'Thailand' (aside from something you might find in the second Hangover movie), is a wooden boat floating peacefully in an impossibly blue ocean, Thai flag fixed to the bow, lonely cliffs rising dramatically out of the water behind it. Chances are, that photo was taken in the south.

Beaches, islands, hammocks, cocktails, spectacular national parks, forests, waterfalls, wildlife.

Every tourist's dream compressed into one Thai region, basically.

Climate

If you had an idea that Thailand was always hot and sunny, we've got good news for you. You were half-right!

It's a pretty big country, so of course there's some regional differences in the climate, but let's not get too bogged down in that. To summarize: the weather swings are more pronounced in the north, and far less severe in the south.

Thailand's weather can be broken down into three main seasons:

1) The 'cool season' runs from November to February. What it should be called is the 'slightly cooler than the rest of the year season', but we admit that's not as snappy. Temperatures usually range from 18 and 32 degrees, with minimal humidity. If you can make it work for you, this is the best time to visit.

2) Then comes the hot season. From March until June temperatures can regularly hit 40 degrees, with high levels of humidity. If you visit during this season, things are going to get very sticky very fast. Don't let that put you off, though: it's tolerable, just not so comfortable.

3) Finally, from July until October, there's the rainy season. When they say rainy, they definitely mean rainy. Temperatures are similar to the cool season, but it rains almost every day, without fail. This shouldn't scare you off visiting, however; the downpours may be torrential but they're also brief, usually only lasting a couple of hours.

Whenever you visit, make no mistake; you're going to want your Ray-Bans. Whatever the season you can usually rely on the sun to shine through. Rainy season tends to be greyer, but in the hot and cool seasons you can go days at a time with hardly a cloud in the sky.

Some of you may have just broken your iPad, passing out with boredom and cracking your head on the screen as soon as you saw the word 'history'. Don't worry; we'll keep it short, sharp and painless.

In fact, we'll even say 'Did you know?' before each point; that always makes learning things more interesting!

- Did you know *the area we now know and love as 'Thailand' has been inhabited for as long as Asia has been civilized? There's some dispute as to whether the first residents were Chinese who migrated south, or whether there were already native people in the area. We'll leave that one to the scholars, but the key point is that there were people were there.*

- Did you know *Thailand has had 4 different capitals? The first was Sukhothai (1238-1378), then Ayutthaya (1350-1767), followed by Thonburi (1767-1782), and finally Bangkok (1782-the exact moment you're reading this!). For more information on visiting Thailand, check out our fifth chapter on central Thailand.*

- Did you know *Thailand and neighboring Burma fought on and off for a whopping 308 years (1547-1855). The good news is that they get along royally now, aside from the odd border dispute here and there.*

- Did you know *(speaking of 'royally') the Chakri dynasty began in Thailand 1782, and is still in place today? Some of the more notable throne-dwellers were Rama I, who moved the capital to Bangkok in the first place; Rama V, who developed relationships with Europe and the USA; and the late, great Rama IX, who, before his death in October 2016, had donned the crown for an impressive 70 years.*

- Did you know *that Muang Thai (Thailand, to you and us), has only been the country's name since 1939? Before that it was known as Siam. Myth busted: if your mate told you Thailand meant 'Land of the Free', as many people think, he or she is a misinformed fool! It actually means – you guessed it – 'Land of Thais'.*

- Did you know *Thailand is the only country in the region never to have been colonized by a European power? As Britain, France and the Netherlands were carving up the countries around them, the sly Thais maintained cordial relations with everybody, and kept their autonomy.*

- Did you know *Thailand had an absolute monarchy right up until 1932, when it was replaced by a parliamentary government in a peaceful coup?*

- *OK, so we've got on to coups.* Did you know *that Thailand has had more coups in contemporary history than any other country in the world? Since 1932 there have been 19 attempts, 12 of which have been successful. The most recent was in 2014, when General Prayut Chan-o-cha overthrew Yingluck Shinawatra's government (Bonus fact: Yingluck was the country's first female prime minister, and is the sister of former Manchester City FC owner (oh, and prime minster of Thailand) Thaksin Shinawatra).*

And that just about brings us up to present. See, that wasn't too painful was it? You there, at the back of the class; wake up!

Thailand's official economy is called 'baht'. The end.

Only joking! We've dug deep behind the sofa cushion, rummaged around, and pulled out a few shiny facts in which you can invest your attention.

- *Thailand has the second biggest economy in Southeast Asia, topped only by Indonesia (which does have around 186 million more people), and the 28th biggest in the entire world.*

- *Exports make up more than 2/3 of Thailand's economy. The main goods they export include computers, cars, jewelry and rice.*

- *Speaking of rice! Growing rice was the historical bedrock of Thailand's economy. It's not quite as dominant as it once was, however; despite 50% of employment being agricultural, this only makes up 10% of the country's economic output.*

- *Manufacturing and trade have far outstripped agriculture now, each making up around 1/5 of the economy.*

- *Thailand has made huge strides in reducing poverty in the past few decades. In 1986 67% of the population lived in poverty; by 2014 that number had fallen massively, to 11%.*

- *There's a big imbalance between the cities and the countryside, with 80% of those still in poverty living in rural areas.*

- *Thailand has one of the world's lowest unemployment rates, at less than 1%. Impressive!*

- *A minimum wage was introduced in 2013, ensuring workers would earn a minimum of 300 baht (around $10), per day.*

2. What Makes Thailand Tick?

In the last chapter we gave you a 30,000ft view of Thailand as we soared over it, covering the macro facts about the country and its past. In this chapter, we're going to swoop ever closer to Thailand as we prepare for our landing. We'll be looking at what really makes the country tick: its people.

We'll be covering their **culture and religion**, with some tips following on for **what to do and what not to do**. We'll look at the Thai **language**, including a few basic phrases for you to master. Finally we will, of course, be looking at the **food**, and highlighting a few must-try dishes.

Let's get to it!

We've included culture and religion together because they're so inextricably linked.

Thailand has complete religious freedom, with people free to practice whatever they desire. While there is a significant minority of Muslims, especially in the south, Buddhism is still the dominant religion. Over 93% of Thais are Buddhist (Theravada Buddhists, specifically). The country contains over 27,000 temples where, as well as worshipping, people can also seek medical help and counselling from the resident monks.

The basic foundations of Buddhism – to treat others with compassion and care for them, to be honest, to avoid conflict, and so on – are evident in the everyday behavior of Thai people. The Thais are renowned for their friendliness, politeness, and always showing a level of respect to each other and to foreigners, and the role that religion plays in this is significant.

Thai society is generally hierarchical. Younger people are expected to be especially respectful to their elders, children to their parents, workers to their bosses; and the royal family – at the top of the hierarchy – are to be revered by everybody.

Thailand has a number of traditional yearly celebrations, which are big social occasions where huge numbers of Thai people come together, as well as being significant religiously. We've included a breakdown of some of the country's biggest and most spectacular festivals later on in the book. This will help you out if you want to time your visit to match with one of them, to make your stay in Thailand especially memorable.

What to do, and what not to do

The Thai people are, widely-speaking, pretty easy-going. They're extremely approachable, and always willing to engage in a bit of joking around, whether you speak the same language or not!

Tourism is a massive industry in Thailand. The chances are that residents of major cities and tourist destinations, from Phuket right up to Chiang Mai, will have seen it all when it comes to visitors to their country. If you accidentally fail to follow their customs, they're very unlikely to start shouting at you on the street.

This is doubly true because Thais are so polite. Even if you do something that is completely culturally inappropriate, they'll almost certainly hold their tongue. Don't think, just because you're not constantly being corrected, that your behavior is perfect.

Being the good tourists that you are, we know that you'll want to follow the customs of Thailand as closely as you possibly can! Here's a breakdown of some of the main things that you should, and definitely should not do, on your visit to Thailand.

- **Do** dress appropriately

A general expectation is that clothing should cover shoulders and knees. Of course, this is a rule that's broken almost constantly by tourists. If you've been in a major tourist area for over five minutes, the chances are you will have seen girls walking around in tiny shorts, and guys strutting about in vests.

The only places where it's completely necessary to follow this rule, are temples and palaces. If your knees or shoulders are exposed, you probably won't even be allowed inside. To cover up your knees, make sure you bring trousers with you, or a sarong. For your shoulders, just wear a t-shirt, or bring along a jacket.

Many of the main temples and palaces, such as The Grand Palace in Bangkok, will have clothing available to borrow if you've forgotten to dress appropriately, but don't bank on finding this everywhere.

On the beaches, you can wear your normal swimwear. The Thais won't be joining you, as they have a strong aversion to tanning, but they're contented to let the farangs (foreigners) have their fun!

- **Don't** expect everybody to know English

Thailand has made enormous strides in recent decades to become a powerful economical country, and a respected member of the international community. This doesn't mean, however, that everybody speaks English.

Generally speaking, you'll be fine in major destinations like Bangkok, Chiang Mai, Phuket, and so on. You'll encounter plenty of Thais, often working in restaurants or bars, whose English is excellent. Your average man or woman on the street, however, might not be so comfortable.

As the economy has grown, education in Thailand has developed with it, with most Thai students being taught at least a basic grasp of English at school. This means that, if you find yourself in a rural area away from the major tourist hubs, you've got a better chance communicating with younger people.

- **Do** *learn some Thai*

Of course, instead of depending on the Thai people to know English, you could put a little time into learning their language! You might not be able to learn enough to hold a proper conversation before you begin your trip, but you can easily pick up a few basic phrases.

Thai people love to hear foreigners attempting to speak their language, and are often complimentary of your lingual skills (even if you're positive that they're terrible!). If you're planning to stay in Thailand for a long time, learning the language is a mark of cultural respect, as it is for immigrants in every country.

To learn a few key words and phrases, head over to our next section in this chapter, 'Language'.

- **Don't** *be loud*

Loudness, unless it's completely necessary, is considered rude in Thailand. Any place you go where the majority of people are locals, whether it be a restaurant or on a Skytrain in Bangkok, you're likely to be struck by how relatively quiet the place is.

This is one of the many ways in which tourists stick out from everybody else. Try to do as the Thai people do: even if you're in a big group, and however excited you are to be on your way to your first Muay Thai fight – or however many Chang beers you've had – try to keep your voice down.

- **Do** *be patient*

Whilst Thailand's economy has developed enormously, there are still a few things that might frustrate you on your first visit to Thailand. The traffic in big cities is almost always terrible, and public transportation – buses especially – rarely leaves when it's supposed to and can get severely overbooked. As we mentioned earlier, there's often still a major language barrier in place, meaning ordering at restaurants or asking where something is can sometimes become a drawn-out process.

Above all, always remember that you're a guest in their country, and that the Thai people are probably doing their best to help. Just take a page out of their book, and – whatever happens – just keep on smiling!

- **Don't** count on the police

We're sure you won't need this tip, but we'll leave it here just in case! You should be extra careful with regards to getting into any kind of altercation with a local. If something serious does happen, and the police are called, they will almost certainly take their follow countryperson's side.

Even if a Thai person isn't involved, dealing with the police can prove difficult and, in particular, costly. The Thai police have a widespread reputation for being quite corrupt, which isn't entirely without merit. Whatever the offence, there have been a large number of reports of police demanding payments from you on the spot, in exchange for not taking things further.

Drug offences, as you might have heard, are taken extremely seriously in Thailand. Even simple possession or use of drugs can land you a hefty sentence, in terms of money or even jail time. Thai jails are no joke so, for the sake of safety, the best advice we can offer you is simply to not take the risk!

- **Do** respect monks

Monks are extremely highly respected in Thai society, being seen almost as role models. Thai people consider it a fundamental part of their civic duty to donate often to monks and monasteries in order to sustain them.

They don't behave in a haughty, superior way though. You'll see monks walking around the streets and riding on buses just like normal people. They're even often willing to enter into conversation with foreigners they meet.

Simply treat them with the respect that the rest of Thai society does, by allowing them to pass by you easily on the street, for example, and you'll be fine.

One word of warning. Women are not allowed to touch monks in Buddhist societies, so if you see a monk walking towards you, give him an extra-wide berth!

- **Don't** point your feet

Feet are considered the least important and dirtiest part of the body, particularly because they're the furthest point from the head, which is the most spiritually important part.

Whenever you're sitting down, be extra-careful not to point your feet at anyone: it's considered a mark of disrespect, and a huge faux-pas if your feet are point at a Buddha image or statue. Never stretch your legs out in front of you. Instead, cross them beneath you, or kneel.

- **Do** take your shoes off

Talking of feet! There are plenty of situations in Thailand when you'll be expected to remove your shoes when you enter a building. This will always be the case when you enter a temple, and is usually true when you visit a Thai person's home too.

People may also remove their shoes in other situations, such as when they visit certain restaurants, or enter certain buildings in a school. Don't panic, though! A good habit to get into is doing a quick check when you go into a building, and seeing if there's a shoe rack by the door, or if everyone else who's already inside has their shoes off. If not, you're probably OK!

- **Don't** point with your fingers

This isn't the most heinously disrespectful thing you can do, but pointing with your fingers is still considered to be an aggressive gesture.

If you need to do a bit of beckoning, whether it's for the waiter in a restaurant or for a taxi driver, don't hold your hand aloft with your fingers up. Instead, hold your arm out horizontally with the palm of your hand facing downwards, and with your fingers pointing towards the ground.

- **Do** smile!

Thailand is known as the Land of Smiles for good reason. If you've never visited before, you'll be pleasantly surprised by just how many teeth are on show!

Thai people have a smile for every occasion. In fact, it's been calculated that Thai people have a total of thirteen different smiles, each suitable for a different occasion. They have pleasant smiles, for admiring somebody's accomplishment or for simply feeling happy. They also have... less pleasant smiles. These can be used to mock people, or when they're feeling sad.

The important thing is that they smile a lot! Follow suit. Whatever situation you find yourself in, or whoever you're talking to, a smile can often work wonders and make an especially good impression. Plus, smiling is supposed to be good for your health, you know.

- **Don't** disrespect the monarchy

This is an especially important one, which you need to follow at all times.

Plenty of countries respect their monarchs, but in Thailand they take it a step further. Criticizing or gossiping about the monarchy is actually illegal, punishable by a jail term of up to fifteen years.

Don't think that you'll be excused just because you're a tourist. Plenty of foreigners have been jailed over the years for perceived slights against the royals. Thailand may be an extremely welcoming country to foreign people, but they (and more importantly their judicial system) draw the line at the royal family.

- **Do** respect a person's personal space

Thai people don't have the same rules of physical contact that many western countries do. While locals will often shake your hand, especially if they're well-acquainted with receiving tourists, it's not a natural Thai greeting (a simple 'savadee-kap' for men, or 'savadee-ka' for women, will usually suffice; if you want to be respectful, put your hands together as if you're praying, and nod your head to the other person).

As we mentioned, the head is considered the most spiritual place in the body, so you should never touch another person's head. Also, make sure you never walk over a person's legs or feet, if they're sitting down; it's considered very rude, and it's not so hard to simply walk around them instead!

- **Don't** neglect your personal hygiene!

When it comes to hygiene, the Thais are almost obsessive. They'll usually have at least two showers per day – one when they wake up, and another before they go to bed – and always wear fresh clothes, to name just two examples.

In a country as hot as Thailand, where you're likely to start sweating from the moment you leave your hotel room, it's especially important that you follow suit! If you start smelling a bit… musty, you'll stick out like a sore thumb.

The most commonly spoken language in Thailand is – you guessed it – Thai! Not our most interesting fact, we'll admit.

Thai is a complex and nuanced language. The same word can have a multitude of meanings depending on how it's said. The word 'mai', for example can mean 'wood', 'not', 'silk', 'burn' or 'new' depending on the inflection. You'd better make sure you know exactly how to pronounce a word before you try speaking to a local, if you want to avoid a swift slap around the face (that's a joke, just for the record; if you want to try some Thai, go for it!).

Much like French, Italian, Spanish and Portuguese all share a common ancestry as 'romance languages', Thai comes from the Tai-Kadai family of speech, the variations of which are spoken by nearly 100 million people. The most commonly spoken by far are Thai and Lao. While the languages are different, the residents of these neighboring countries can broadly understand each other.

There are actually five official variations of spoken Thai, each suitable for a different occasion. Common Thai and formal Thai are the most commonly spoken (both pretty self-explanatory). There's also rhetorical Thai, which is used for making public speeches; religious Thai, for speaking to monks, or about Buddhism generally; and royal Thai, used to discuss the royal family, or on the off chance that you bump into a member of the royal family. There's a type of Thai for every occasion!

Spoken Thai is hard enough to grasp, but when it comes to written Thai… you might as well give up now. Maybe that sounds a little negative, but just head on Google Images and take a look at some, and tell us we're wrong!

There's a lot to learn, for starters, with the Thai alphabet dwarfing our Latin version. They have 44 consonants and 15 vowels, compared to our measly 21 and 5. As you may have noticed if you've ever looked at written Thai, they don't put spaces between words in a sentence; that's one of the reasons why it looks so daunting.

If you do want to have a crack at learning it, we have some good news for you. Like English, Thai is an alphabetic language, meaning that when you learn to recognize the characters you'll be able to say the words. This is in contrast to Chinese, for example, which is 'logographic', meaning that a single symbol represents a whole word. (Incidentally, if you thought the idea of learning Thai was daunting with all those letters, the average Chinese person has to memorize over 4,000 characters. It could be worse!).

The standard of spoken English in Thailand varies wildly from place to place. Generally speaking, you'll be fine in the bigger, more touristic towns and cities. In the countryside, you might have to resort to charades, or at least a lot of pointing.

Just in case you need it, or simply for a bit of fun, take the time to learn some Thai before you head out there. You can find plenty of helpful videos on the internet to help you with pronunciation, but here are a few of the key words and phrases to store away before you begin your journey:

(Note: some words differ depending on whether you are male or female, not whether the person you're talking to is)

Hello – Sa-va-dee-kap (male)/ Sa-va-dee-ka (female)

Thank you – Kap-kun-kap (male)/ Kap-kun-ka (female)

Yes – Chai

No – Mai

Beer – Bia

Please – Ga roo nah

I can't speak Thai – Pood Thai mai dai

One – neung

Two – song

Three – sam

Four – see

Five – haa

Ten – seep

One hundred – roy

3. Thailand's 10 Must-See Attractions

So we've taken our sky-high view of Thailand, then begun our descent with a more in-depth look at its inhabitants. Now, it's time to get even closer, and take a look at some of the essential parts of any visit to the Land of Smiles.

Thailand is a large country, which continually rewards your efforts at exploration with throwing up new hidden gems, and unexpected experiences. We'll take a deeper look into all the major locations and more in the coming chapters. For now, however, we want to draw your attention to 10 things in Thailand that you definitely can't afford to miss.

These are the 10 truly must-see things in Thailand, which absolutely must be part of any visitor's itinerary.

1) The Grand Palace -- Bangkok

If you want to see classical Thai architecture at its most bejeweled, and its most opulent, look no further than the Grand Palace. If Bangkok is the beating heart of Thailand, then the Grand Palace is the heart of Bangkok.

It's the official residence of the Thai royal family, and has been for over 230 years. The royal family may no longer actually live here, but it's still the center for the most important national events.

It's situated in Bangkok's old town, right on the banks of the Chao Phraya river. You'll be able to find it easily enough: as soon as you get within a square mile of it, just start following the hordes of tourists and the big tour buses. It's almost always busy inside, but this won't spoil your experience. A visit is still absolutely worth it.

The complex is enormous, with so many amazing buildings and wall murals that you'll lose track of them all. If you want a crash course in how important the royal family are to the Thai people, look no further than this place.

At the center of everything, and almost certainly your highlight of the visit, is Wat Phra Kaew; better known to tourists as the Temple of the Emerald Buddha. The Emerald Buddha itself, needless to say, is the stunning centerpiece of the temple. The exterior of the building is extremely impressive too, though. The peak of the spire above the temple is visible from far away, and the outside walls are covered in gold and expertly carved mystical figures.

Make no mistake: the Grand Palace should be your first stop in Bangkok, and maybe in all of Thailand.

2) Wat Phra That Doi Suthep -- Chiang Mai

Looming over the hipster haven of Chiang Mai, right up in the north of Thailand, is Doi Suthep. This majestic mountain is visible from almost everywhere in the city and, standing atop it like a shining beacon, is the golden temple: Wat Phra That.

The distance from the city center, and the steepness of the mountain, means that walking is pretty much out of the question for everyone who isn't a professional athlete. Drive up there if you've got a car, or take one of the ubiquitous red taxis which you'll see cruising around.

Either way, you'll reach the car park near the peak of the mountain, and climb up a few hundred steep steps. You'll be a little sweaty by the time you reach the top, but we promise it'll be worth it.

The highlight of this trip isn't actually the temple, although it's still worth looking around. The reason you make the journey is for the view. On the far side of the temple from the road, there's a viewpoint which will take your breath away.

The whole of Chiang Mai is laid out before you, and you can see the green mountain falling away from you on either side. It's a view – and a moment in your trip to Thailand – that you'll never forget.

3) Terminal 21 - Bangkok

In truth, there are so many enormous and unique shopping malls in Bangkok that it was hard to pick only one. The most unique of them all, however, is surely Terminal 21.

The atrium into which you enter Terminal 21 is designed to look like – you guessed it – an airport terminal. Go further inside, and you might start to notice something a little different about the design.

Every floor in Terminal 21 is designed to look like a city in a different country. London, Rome, Tokyo and San Francisco are just some of the cities you can visit, all in one building. It's still a mall, so the whole place is made up of shops and restaurants.

They've gone to a huge amount of effort, however, and paid close attention to detail, to make sure that every floor has a different feeling. Even the bathrooms have been designed to resemble parts of the different countries: on the British floor, for example, the bathrooms look as if you're on the London Underground.

The shops themselves are also delightful. They aren't the enormous chains that you'll find in most shopping malls: Gap, Topshop, H&M and so on. They're more independent, and their goods are creative and lovingly crafted.

If you only have time to visit one shopping mall in Bangkok, and you're looking for a unique shopping experience, choose Terminal 21.

4) The Sanctuary of Truth - Pattaya

The Sanctuary of Truth, in Pattaya, is a large temple – with the spire being over 100m high – that's made entirely out of wood. It looks spectacular enough from far away: it's right next to the beach, so as you approach you can see the ocean in the background.

When you get closer, though, you understand just how much work has gone into the building. The place is covered in intricate sculptures which have been hand-carved out of wood. Work is actually still continuing – the temple isn't expected to be completed until 2050 – so when you visit you're likely to see the skilled craftsmen still at work on their carvings.

The chances are that you're going to see a lot of temples during your time in Thailand. There are the famous ones, like the aforementioned Wat Phra That on Doi Suthep, and then there are ones you'll stumble across as you explore the cities and the countryside. Wherever you go in Thailand, however, or maybe in all of Asia, you're unlikely to find one quite like this.

5) The Elephants

Elephants are as synonymous with Thailand as anything. If you've got a friend who went away to Thailand and came back with a present for you, we're 80% sure it was a carved mini elephant!

You'll have plenty of opportunities to ride on the back of an elephant in the more touristic areas, but to see them in a more natural habitat, and at their happiest, we'd recommend going to an elephant park.

There are lots of great ones dotted around the country, with the Elephant Nature Park near Chiang Mai being particularly excellent. Whichever elephant park you go to, you'll find elephants roaming around vast green pastures, bathing in rivers, or rolling around in the mud. You'll have the opportunity to get up close and personal with these majestic beasts and, of course, get a photo with one for your Instagram!

This is yet another of those amazing opportunities that you have in Thailand to make a memory for life.

6) The White Temple – Chiang Rai

The Sanctuary of Truth is really something, but Wat Rong Khun – better known to tourists as the White Temple – might just be even more unique.

If you've done any prior research into Thailand, you will almost certainly have seen Wat Rong Khun. It is – as its adopted English name suggests – a temple which is completely white. The exterior design is particularly complex and striking, even for a Thai temple.

The inside of the temple is even more unusual than the outside, and that's saying something! We don't want to spoil the surprise for you, but it's well worth the entry fee.

7) Erawan Falls – Kanchanaburi

Thailand is blessed with an enormous number of natural treasures, but Erawan Falls is certainly one of the best.

Set in Erawan National Park, the waterfall is actually separated into seven different tiers, each with its own waterfall. The first three are easily accessible, then to reach the rest you need to hike through the thick, beautiful forest. Don't worry about getting too sweaty on your climb, because you can take a refreshing dip in the cool, fresh pools of water beneath the falls.

Erawan National Park is an easy day trip from Bangkok, with bookings available from any number of tourist agencies, hostels and hotels.

This is a popular spot with tourists and Thais alike, with everyone enjoying a splash around. It's a great chance to see some of Thailand's beautiful nature, and have a lot of fun at the same time!

8) Bridge on the River Kwai – Kanchanaburi

The 'Death Railway' was built under brutal working conditions by prisoners of war during World War Two. The most well-known section is, of course, Bridge 277, made famous by the Hollywood movie 'The Bridge on the River Kwai'.

The Bridge is located in Kanchanaburi Province, and can easily be seen in a day trip on the way to Erawan Falls. There are some great museums to check out in the nearby town if you want to learn more about the history of the region.

Thanks mostly to the movie (and also the focus of another, more recent Hollywood movie, 'The Railway Man'), this is one of the most internationally famous things to visit in the country, and a must-see on your Thailand bucket list.

9) The Beach – Ko Phi Phi

Let's stay on the Hollywood movie theme! Did you know that you can actually visit 'the beach', from the Leonardo DiCaprio movie 'The Beach'? It's a dream come true for any movie buff! The beach in question is located in Thailand's sumptuous south, on the island of Ko Phi Phi.

Ko Phi Phi is basically a must-see on its own, but we wanted to identify a specific experience for you! The beach itself is in Maya Bay and, while it may not look exactly the same as it did in the movie, you can still see why the filmmakers chose this location to represent a new paradise. Perfect golden sand and blue waters surrounded by mountains... Thailand's south doesn't get much more picturesque than this.

A trip there is easily booked from the main parts of Koh Phi Phi, and will only set you back around 400 baht for the half-day. That sounds like pretty good value to us!

10) A Muay Thai fight

Along with elephants, blue waters and beach parties, the combat sport Muay Thai is surely one of the main things you think of when you think about Thailand.

It's basically Thailand's national sport: as you walk around you'll see innumerable posters advertising the latest fights, and plenty of gyms where fighters train (and where you can even have a go yourself, if you're brave enough!).

Every major settlement will offer the chance to see Muay Thai fights, although the quality is obviously greater in the big cities, where the crowds and money at stake are at their highest. In the capital Bangkok, Lumpini Stadium is arguably the most prestigious arena in the entire country, whilst Rajadamnern Stadium has a storied history over its many decades of existence. If you're in the south, we'd recommend heading to Patong Boxing Stadium in Phuket, or if you're up in the north Thaphae Stadium in Chiang Mai is definitely worth a visit.

To be completely honest, unless you're a combat sports expert yourself, you're unlikely to notice the difference in quality between the various stadia. If you can't make it to one of the biggest venues, just go and watch a fight wherever you can! Watching Muay Thais is simply about soaking up one of the most popular and authentic local Thai experiences.

4. Central Thailand: The Country's Beating Heart

We've gotten to know Thailand from up high – its layout, its history, its people – and we've brought you the 10 things which you absolutely must visit. Now it's time to zoom in more, and look at the three main regions of Thailand.

We'll begin with the middle; the heart of Thailand. Everything begins, of course, with Bangkok. The capital city is far and away the biggest settlement in the country, the home to the royal family and the government, and the place where trends are made. This has been the case for centuries: the vast majority of the main Thai dishes you know and love, like green curry and Tom Yam soup, originated in the central region. The chances are, when you're eating Thai food, you're eating something originating from a central recipe.

There's plenty more to the middle of the country, however. In this section we'll look first at Bangkok, then move on to the region's other two main destinations: Pattaya and Ayutthaya.

Bangkok

What to Know

Where do we even start? With a population of over 8million people in the central area, and 14.5million in the metropolitan area, Bangkok doesn't sound like an especially big capital city. Not when you compare it some of the others in the region, anyway; Jakarta, the Indonesian capital, has over 30million people in its metropolitan area. When you're actually in Bangkok though, it feels enormous.

This is a sprawling urban jungle, with dozens of different areas each with their own characteristics. Phra Nakhon is the supposed 'old town' (although Bangkok is such a modern, fast-moving city that you'll struggle to find many truly old buildings, even there), home to the Grand Palace and lots of the larger temples. Sukhumvit is the city center, where cavernous shopping malls and parks abound. Plenty of more suburban, quieter neighborhoods border Sukhumvit, such as Samut Prakan and Chatuchak.

There's something in Bangkok for everyone. You hear this a lot about cities, but it's not always true; with Bangkok, it most certainly is. Walks in the park, drinks on the roof of a skyscraper, shopping binges, clubbing, museum visits, theme parks... you name it, and we almost guarantee you'll be able to do it in Bangkok.

Areas

Getting around the city is also extremely easy. Taxis are ubiquitous, although the frequently congested traffic means they're not always the best option: make sure you check Google Maps for live traffic updates before you commit to a ride, or your costs could start to skyrocket. Buses around town are frequent, incredibly cheap, and will get you basically anywhere you'd like to go. Most pleasant of all is the BTS Skytrain: a rail system built on tracks high above the city streets. It's also inexpensive, it's very reliable, and you swoop easily over all the traffic below you. Likewise, the underground Metro system will quickly get you where you need to go, and keep you off the roads.

How long should you spend in Bangkok? Well, how long have you got? You can tick off the main tourist sites within a few days, but the longer you spend there, and the more areas you explore, the more you'll grow to love the place.

We know that travelers aren't always lucky enough to be able to spend as long as they like in a place, however. That's why we've put together a list of some of the things you should definitely build into your Bangkok itinerary.

What to See

The Grand Palace

We mentioned this in our '10 Must-See Attractions' section, but it really is an absolutely essential stop on your Bangkok visit. The complex is vast, and the place is so detailed and spectacular that you'll want at least two hours there to truly take it all in, and take all the photos you need.

The Grand Palace is open every day, but please note that it closes at 3:30pm, so make sure you don't get there too late!

Lumphini Park

Lumphini Park manages the amazing achievement of making you completely forget that you're in the middle of a thriving, bustling city.

It's a large park, set right in the heart of the city near Sukhumvit Road, the city's main thoroughfare. There are grassy areas to chill out on, large lakes with benches to sit and relax on, sculptures to study, running lanes, and plenty more. There are even giant lizards which slowly crawl along on the grass, or lazily swim through the water. It's basically a perfect park!

If you are getting slightly overwhelmed by the big city, Lumphini Park is where you should go to unwind.

Wat Pho

If the Grand Palace is a filling main course, then Wat Pho is a perfect dessert. It's basically located right across the street, a very short walk away. While it isn't a small place, it's far less epic than the Grand Palace, and the crowds are significantly smaller.

It's pleasant to walk around the complex and enjoy the colorful stupas, but the main attraction of Wat Pho is its reclining Buddha.

Situated in a hall of its own, this reclining Buddha is absolutely huge (a whopping 45m long), and is covered in gold. It's majestic, and stunning to look at.

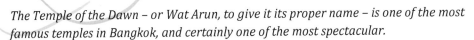

The Temple of the Dawn

The Temple of the Dawn – or Wat Arun, to give it its proper name – is one of the most famous temples in Bangkok, and certainly one of the most spectacular.

It's easily combined with your visits to The Grand Palace and Wat Pho: just head west across the street from Wat Pho, go through a covered market, and you'll reach a pier (called Tha Tien). From there you'll see Wat Arun's huge, grey prang (the main tower), dramatically dominating the view across the river. It's a quick and cheap (only 3 baht) boat ride across the river to reach the temple.

Once there you can enter the complex for free, strolling around the expertly-maintained gardens and peeking inside some of the outer buildings. There's a 50 baht charge to get inside the main part of the compound, but it's more than worth it to inspect the intricate porcelain decorations of the temple up close.

If you judge the fame of a tourist destination based purely on how many postcards you see it on while you walk around, Wat Arun is definitely up there; in fact, it might be second only to The Grand Palace. Don't miss the opportunity to see this iconic structure for yourself, especially when it feeds so effortlessly into your tour of the old town.

The Golden Mount

Wat Saket – better known to foreigners as the Golden Mount – is located in Bangkok's old town. It's around a thirty minute walk from the Grand Palace, so if you're thinking of trying to see all the main sites in the old town in one day (which is difficult, but certainly possible), we'd recommend getting a taxi or a tuk tuk over there.

The complex really does resemble a small mountain, albeit one which has its sides painted in white and with a golden temple on top. The walk up the path, which circles the main building and gradually climbs, is delightful. You're accompanied by flowing water and the sounds of bells chiming in the breeze as you ascend. The climb isn't taxing at all, and when you reach the top you're rewarded with a nice view over the surrounding area, as well as the golden prang which gives the place its name.

The Shopping Malls

Bangkok is home to a frankly ridiculous number of shopping malls, with something to cater to everyone's taste and budget. We already mentioned Terminal 21 in a previous chapter, and that certainly is the most unique of the bunch, but there are a few others that deserve a mention.

The Emporium might just be the classiest of the bunch. It's a stylishly designed building which is home to some of the biggest names in luxury shopping. There's also a very nice viewpoint higher up the building, an excellent cinema, and even a waterfall which pours down through the higher levels.

The Bangkok Art and Culture Centre isn't quite as unique as Terminal 21, but it's certainly an unusual space. It's half shopping mall, half art gallery. There are lovely little arts and crafts shop on each level, but also photography exhibits and paintings hanging from the walls.

Finally, another great one to check out, especially if you're looking to pick up a bargain, is the MBK Center, which is just across the street from the Art and Culture Center. It's a big step down in terms of price from The Emporium, with hundreds of shops wedged in tightly next to each other, offering all the clothing, beauty products, and so on that you *could possibly desire. The MBK Center is also home to a state of the art multiplex cinema, as well as a great arcade!*

Khao San Road

No guide to Bangkok is complete without a mention of the infamous Khao San Road. It's the party capital of Thailand, and probably of Southeast Asia.

It's certainly not for everyone. If your idea of an enjoyable night out is a glass of fine wine in a nice bar, perhaps with a little piano music in the background, Khao San is not for you. It's squarely aimed at backpackers and everyone else who wants to get very drunk, and listen to music that's very loud.

It's certainly an extremely fun time if you're in the right mood, but if you're not... well, don't say we didn't warn you!

Pattaya

What to Know

Pattaya is easily the number one beach destination in central Thailand. It's a comfortable three hour journey by car from Bangkok, and it's got everything you could want from a coastal city: restaurants galore, including plenty of seafood; seemingly infinite bars; and, of course, beaches!

Pattaya has acquired a... reputation, as being something of a seedy place. Those elements are there of course: there are certain streets which seemed to be filled exclusively with go-go bars, where drunken single tourists pass their evenings talking to beautiful Thai girls dressed in skimpy clothes. If this is your kind of thing, then Pattaya is the place for you!

There is another side to it, though. The beaches are expansive, extending most of the way along the coastline, and they aren't usually too overcrowded. If you want somewhere to chill out in a deckchair with a cocktail, and to go for a nice swim, but you haven't got time to go all the way to the south, Pattaya is definitely worth checking out. You can also engage in all the watersports you could desire, from jet skiing, to windsurfing, to diving.

There's a huge range of hotels, which range, depending on your budget, from basic to luxurious. There are also quieter parts of town to explore outside of the main, quite boisterous center. Even if you find absolutely nothing to enjoy in the city itself – which is unlikely – there are a variety of engaging day trips you can take part in.

What to See

Pattaya Beach

The main reason people visit Pattaya is, of course, for the beach!

Pattaya Beach is the main one in the city. It's fairly big, at around 3km long, which means you should have no trouble finding a spot. It's easily accessible from basically anywhere, whether you choose to take a private taxi, a communal taxi (called a 'songthaew'), or rent a motorbike or a bicycle.

Get there nice and early, before most of the other tourists, and pick which deckchair you want. Whichever you choose, you'll be catered to all day by one of the locals, who'll bring you any drink you desire whenever you like (also known as 'being in heaven'). If you're not in the mood to relax, you can arrange any number of watersport activities with one of the many agencies in the city.

The Sanctuary of Truth

We mentioned this in our '10 Must-See Attractions' chapter, but it's worth repeating! If you can possibly spare a couple of hours away from the beach, you should absolutely visit the Sanctuary of Truth (known in Thai as Wang Boran).

We're guessing you've never seen a giant Buddhist temple made of wood, right next to a beach, before; and you never know when you might see one again! Make sure to pay it a visit while you're in Pattaya.

Walking Street

If you are interested in seeing Pattaya's slightly seedier side, or you're just craving a big night out, head to the Walking Street!

It's situated right in the city center, and runs parallel to Pattaya Tai Beach. Don't worry about not being able to find it, though: you'll be able to hear it before you see it, and if not you can just follow the crowds!

It's definitely the chief nightlife spot in the city. It's packed to bursting point with bars, both regular and go-go, and the whole place is flooded with neon lighting at nighttime, when it almost seems to become one big, bustling party.

Ramayana Water Park

'Why would I go to a water park, when I'm right next to the beach?' we hear you ask. Well, because Ramayana Water Park is even more fun than the beach, and the beach doesn't have water slides!

It's located a short distance south of the main part of the city, and has a reputation as being not just the biggest water park in Thailand, but one of the biggest in Southeast Asia.

It's a great place to take kids, if you've brought them along on the trip (especially because they offer discounted tickets for families), but if you're childless you shouldn't let that stop you! There are 21 different rides, of varying degrees of extremity, and relaxing water pools to chill in if you need to calm down from the excitement.

Nong Nooch Garden

If you've been in Pattaya a few days, and you're after something completely different, consider a day trip out of the city to Nong Nooch Garden.

Believe us when we say this is not the kind of garden that you have at the back of your house. This botanical garden covers an enormous 500 acre area, and has reportedly been named one of the 10 most beautiful gardens in the world.

The area is actually split up into many different sections, including the Italian Garden, Butterfly Hill and even the Cars Garden! There are plenty of unique places to visit in Thailand, but this has to be up there as one of the most unusual, and also one of the most rewarding to visit.

Ayutthaya

What to Know

In a country with a history as rich and storied as Thailand's, it should come as no surprise that there are several fascinating, historical cities to explore. Sukhothai is certainly worth mentioning, and if you have the time you should certainly visit. Sukhothai's location halfway between Bangkok and Chiang Mai makes it the perfect place to stop off for a couple of nights if you're driving up through the country.

We'd like to focus on arguably the most famous and impressive of all, though: Ayutthaya. Its location certainly helps to make it an attractive destination. Situated only 85km or so north of Bangkok, it's a mere ninety minute car or bus journey away. In fact, it's possible to visit as a day trip from the capital city. We'd only recommend this if your time is limited. If you possibly can, and if you have any interest in history whatsoever, you should spare at least a couple of full days to take in everything that Ayutthaya has to offer.

Before modern-day Thailand was a unified country, Ayutthaya was a kingdom all of its own. It was a thriving and extremely powerful one, successfully warring with several of its neighbors, including Sukhothai. At one point, in around 1700, Sukhothai was one of the biggest cities in the world, with a population of over a million people. It was also one of the richest cities in the entire east, and traded extensively with nations all over Asia and Europe.

It remained its own kingdom for over four hundred years, until it was effectively destroyed in a war with Burma in 1767. Today, few of the buildings retain their former structure, but the ruins that are there have been well-preserved.

We've selected a few places in Ayutthaya which we think you should visit. Most of the oldest ruined sites are to be found in the Phra Nakhon Si Ayutthaya Historical Park. A lot of the most impressive ruins are relatively close to each other, and easy to walk between, so we'd recommend simply strolling around and soaking up the atmosphere. To visit Ayutthaya is to take a walk back in time; a thrilling journey through a fallen kingdom.

Wat Phra Manathat

In your research on Thailand, you may have actually seen plenty of photos of Ayutthaya without realizing it. Have you come across the image of the stone Buddha statue's head, fallen to the ground with tree roots growing around it? Well, that was taken in Ayutthaya, at Wat Phra Manthat. If anything symbolizes the mighty former kingdom's fall from grace, and descent back to nature, it's this. For all you budding travel photographers out there, make sure you stop at Wat Phra Manathat!

There are also several tall, stone stupas dotted around the area, which lean precariously to one side, yet somehow manage to stay upright. The rows upon rows of seated Buddha statues which line the walls of the complex are somewhat disconcerting, due to the fact that they're all missing their heads. They are, however, another reminder of Ayutthaya's fall from grace.

As we mentioned, there are lots of places in Ayutthaya's Historical Park that are similar to this; far too many to list individually here. Each of them has something distinct and unique about it though, and you should look to visit as many as you can.

Wat Phra Mongkhon Bophit

There's a truly giant golden Buddha statue to be found in Ayutthaya, which must be seen in person in order to truly appreciate its majesty. It was formerly housed outside the Grand Palace, before being moved to its current location. The original Wat Mongkhon Bophit was burnt down during one of Ayutthaya's many wars, so the current impressively large version is relatively new.

Ayutthaya Historical Study Centre

We've given you a quick crash course into the history of Ayutthaya, but there is much, much more to learn. The place has an absolutely fascinating history; a classic tale of a seemingly unstoppable rise, followed by a terrible fall, with plenty of warring in between.

If we've whetted your appetite, the Historical Study Centre is a great place to learn more. It's very close to the Historical Park itself, and ideally should be visited before you head there: the extra background will give lend more context to your visit, and your experience will be the richer for it.

Chao Phrom Market

Not all of Ayutthaya's delights are centuries-old and ruined! There are lots of great restaurants, as you would expect from any Thai city, and several enjoyable markets to be found.

Chief among them is Chao Phrom Market, which is open every day from 8am until 6pm. The usual clothes and tourist memorabilia are available, but in general it feels more authentic than other markets you'll often find in major tourist destinations. This authenticity is especially evident in the food on offer: you can enjoy a variety of local delicacies, including some delicious curries and Thai/Chinese dishes.

The Dutch Settlement

The Dutch were one of the world's major international trading nations in the 17th century, and, as such a pivotal part of trade in Asia, they obviously set up shop in Ayutthaya. They established a formal trading post in 1608, which gradually grew until it became a full foreign village on Thai soil.

Unfortunately, very little of the original settlement remains today, with the settlement having been destroyed by the Burmese back in 1767. Some of the buildings' foundations are still in place, and a few artefacts have been excavated. What you visit for is the excellent museum, Baan Hollanda. You'll be taught all about the history of the Dutch Settlement in an engaging way. In our modern world, where there's so much talk of globalization and our interconnectedness, it's interesting to learn just how close two countries were, despite geographically being so distant from each other, over 400 years ago.

Most people's journeys in Thailand will begin in Bangkok, with the capital city having the two main international airports in the country. Travelers will then progress northwards or southwards and, if they can afford it of course, they will then take the short flight to Chiang Mai or Phuket.

If you can spare the time, we'd highly discourage you from doing this when you head north. Thailand's main roads are of a high quality, and there are plenty of buses that can take you from one point to the next, or you can easily rent a car. The important thing is to take your time traveling north, along the ground, to truly appreciate the change in scenery.

For the most part, the middle of the country is flat. As you head up through Thailand you notice this gradually starting to change, with the ground on either side of you growing higher and higher. By the time you're truly in the north, you'll find yourself in the mountains. Going by car or bus is the only way to appreciate this change.

In the north you'll generally find a slower, more relaxed pace of life than you would elsewhere in the rest of the country. The weather is also significantly different. The temperature is cooler all year round, much of which is due to the higher elevation, and the rainy season is more pronounced (the main benefit of which is the greenness of the whole region).

Its proximity to Myanmar and Laos also means that, as you get closer to the borders, you'll find a high level of ethnic diversity. Plenty of villages and larger settlement have been heavily influenced by the neighboring countries. Chiang Mai itself actually switched hands between Thailand and Myanmar for several centuries.

The south has the beaches, and the middle of the country has Bangkok and other big settlements, but the north is where you can find the most spectacular nature. Chiang Mai, the north's biggest settlement, is absolutely a must-visit. If you can find the time, though, you should absolutely venture further afield.

In this chapter we'll concentrate mainly on the north's three most appealing tourist destinations: Chiang Mai, Pai and Chiang Rai. We'll focus on the places themselves, but we'll also get into their surroundings. We will, of course, also take a look at the food! For a list of some of the must-try foodie delights to be found in the north, check out the 'What to Eat' section in our Chiang Mai guide.

What to Know

Chiang Mai is truly the jewel of the north.

Chiang Mai Province is the biggest in the region, with a population of over 1.6 million people, and the city itself is the third biggest in Thailand. It has managed to resist that 'big city' feel, however. The cityscape is definitely low-rise and, while traffic can become congested along the main roads, the place never feels overwhelmingly busy.

Its surroundings certainly help to keep you feeling calm. The Doi Suthep mountain oversees the whole city, and within less than thirty minutes of driving you can be completely out of the city and into the surrounding nature.

Chiang Mai centers around the Old City: a square area, separated from the rest of the city by a moat, and surrounded by the remnants of centuries-old fortifications. The vast majority of the tourist attractions are situated here, although if you want to get away from the crowds and into a more chilled-out area, without going too far, we'd recommend a visit to the Nimman area. Here you'll find all the artisan cafes, cultural events and cool bars that you could wish for, in an area far more populated with locals than tourists.

What to See

Wat Phra That Doi Suthep

We talked about this temple, built on the top of Doi Suthep, in more detail in the '10 Mist-See Attractions' chapter. In short, visiting Wat Phra That should be your number one priority in Chiang Mai, even if it's just for the view alone. It's a bit of a hike to get up there, but certainly not one that you'll regret.

Wat Chedi Luang

Wat Chedi Luang is situated right in the heart of the Old City, all of which can be walked around in a day. The assembly hall, in the middle of the complex, is spacious and opulent, and there are intriguing statues towards the back of the complex. The main draw, however, is the ruined chedi.

Sixty meters tall, and originally built back in 1441, the chedi fell victim to an earthquake less than a century after its construction. It still comes across majestically, and has been well-maintained even in its ruined state. The chedi is visible across much of the old city, and looks especially beautiful, and even a little ghostly, when it's lit up at night.

Wat Phra Singh

Wat Phra Singh is located right on the western side of the Old City. While it doesn't quite have the unique centerpiece of Wat Chedi Luang, or the spectacular views of Wat Phra That, it's still the biggest temple in the city. It's older than the others has well, having been built well over 600 years ago, and the vast main hall is certainly impressive.

Hmong Village

As we said in our What to Know section, in the north of Thailand you're always rewarded for going that little bit further for the sake of exploration. That's why, if you've got the time, you shouldn't just stop at Wat Phra That when you ascend the mountain of Doi Suthep.

Carry on along the road (or ask your tour guide/taxi driver to do so), and you'll reach a Hmong Village. The Hmong are an ethnic group who originally came from China, before spreading downwards through Southeast Asia. The village itself is extremely quiet, a far cry from the crowds of tourists you're likely to have encountered at the temple. The main source of income for the inhabitants is making and selling goods to visitors, and you can immediately see the care and creativity that's gone into their wares.

Bhubing Palace

Bhubing Palace is also situated on Doi Suthep; really, you should plan a whole day just for exploring this mountain! You'll find it between the temple and the Hmong Village.

The Palace is the royal family's official residence when visiting Chiang Mai. You can't actually go into the building itself, but that's OK, because the reason people come here is the gardens. They're extensive, brilliantly arranged, and extremely relaxing to walk around.

They're a must-visit for any botanists or general lovers of nature out there, and should definitely be combined with any visit you make to Wat Phra That.

Sunday Night Market Walking Street

Every Sunday, in the late afternoon, the entire main road through the Old City is closed off, and it becomes the Walking Street Market.

It's a truly enormous market, at around 1km along, with stalls wedged in alongside each other the whole way. You'll be wedged in too: make no mistake, it gets extremely busy there, seemingly whether it's the high season for tourism or not.

The crowds mean that it takes a while to get from one side to the other, and you'll be jostled around a fair amount, but if you're looking for a gift for your friends and family back home, this is the place to come to. There's clothing, jewelry, paintings and plenty more on offer, all of it resolutely Thai in nature, of a high quality, and very reasonably priced.

It might not be your most enjoyable experience in Thailand, especially if you don't like big crowds, but it's a rite of passage for any Chiang Mai visitor!

Doi Inthanon National Park

If you're feeling an ache to get out of town and into the nature of the north, Doi Inthanon National Park should be your top choice.

It's known as 'The Roof of Thailand', and is home to the tallest mountain in Thailand: Doi Inthanon itself. The entire place is pretty high up though, ranging between 800m and 2,565m, and it's actually a part of the Himalayan mountain range. That's right: for only a two hour drive out of Chiang Mai, you can say that you've visited the Himalayas!

The entire park stretches across a large area of over 480km², and aside from the main peak there are waterfalls to check out, birds to watch and trails to hike along.

A visit to Doi Inthanon National Park is a relatively quick and easy way to get into some of Thailand's most spectacular northern scenery.

Your range of options for eating in Chiang Mai is basically unlimited. In the Old City, in particular, you can't walk ten meters without seeing another restaurant. Of course all of the Thai favorites that you know and love are widely available, like Pad Thai and green curry. Whilst you're up in the north, however, you should definitely make time to try some local delicacies.

Khao Soi

Khao Soi is almost certainly the most famous dish of northern Thailand. It's a soup made with egg noodles and yellow curry, which comes with usually comes with chicken or beef and all kinds of extras like lime slices and spring onions. They mix everything together in a bowl for you, with the whole thing blending into a soothing, tasty, full-bodied dish.

If it's your last night in Chiang Mai, and for some reason you still haven't sampled any local dishes, this is the one to go for!

Sai Oua

Sai Oua are grilled, spiced lemongrass sausages. You'll find them in plenty of restaurants, and on food carts all around the city too.

Laap Khua Mu

Laap (sometimes spelled Laab) is actually available across a few Asian countries, but in Thailand is only really popular in the north. It's made mostly of minced pork, put into a spicy salad, with plenty of herbs. It's quite a dry dish, but also strangely refreshing!

Kaeng Khanun

Some Thais in the north see this as their equivalent to the popular Som Tam soup dish. It's really more of a blend between curry and soup, but the most exciting thing about it is its main ingredient: jackfruit. Jackfruit is only naturally grown in Asia, and is hard to find across Europe and North America. So, while you're in the north, order a Kaeng Khanun, in the spirit of trying new things!

Kaeng Hang Lei

Perhaps more than any other dish, this exemplifies the complex and long relationship between Thailand's north and its neighboring countries.

Kaeng Hang Lei is actually a Burmese recipe, which over time has become very popular with northern Thais. It's a curry, not particularly spicy, with pork as the main ingredient and a variety of spices within.

Chiang Rai

What to Know

Chiang Rai is the second most populous province in northern Thailand, and is actually the most densely populated. It lies 200km northwest of Chiang Mai (roughly a three hour drive), and is very close to the borders of both Myanmar and Laos, forming the famous Golden Triangle (famous mostly, that is, for the growing and transport of opium between the countries in the past). A hefty 12.5% of the total population of the province is made up of hill tribes – ethnic minority groups from nearby countries – which, as you can imagine, gives the area a very multicultural feel.

The rap on Chiang Rai, to put it bluntly, is that the city isn't really worth visiting except for the White Temple. While the city itself isn't exactly overflowing with must-see places, especially compared to nearby Chiang Mai, this doesn't mean that you shouldn't visit.

The true joys of the province are really to be found outside the city itself. Here you have arguably the most enchanting nature in the region, and plenty of it. When we tell you that there are five different national parks, all within less than 100km of the city, perhaps you'll understand just how stunning Chiang Rai's surroundings are.

Wat Rong Khun

Wat Rong Khun – or The White Temple – is obviously Chiang Rai's most famous attraction. We went over it in some detail in the '10 Must-See Attractions' section, and it really, really is a 'must-see'. However many pictures you see of the exterior online, you should still see the real thing, and see it up close, to properly appreciate it. The interior is different from any other temple you'll find, and is worth the price of entry alone.

Mae Fah Luang Art & Culture Park

That's right, it's time to get cultural!

This is another great place that you can find within Chiang Rai's city limits. The main pavilion is home to plenty of fascinating Buddhist objects, and here you can also find the world's biggest collection of Lanna (a former kingdom of north Thailand) artefacts.

The exhibits are actually only half of the appeal, because the grounds in which they're to be found are wonderful. There are lakes and ponds situated amongst a diverse range of plants and trees, all within a large, meticulously landscaped garden.

Doi Luang National Park

We've said it before, but we'll say it again because it's so amazing: there are five national parks near to Chiang Rai, and more too if you're willing to travel a little further. In truth, they're all quite beautiful, and if you had the time it'd be great to visit each of them. With so much to do, however, time can get tight on a Thailand tour, so sacrifices must be made.

Doi Luang is the closest national park to the city; you can easily get there in ninety minutes or less by car. It's seriously big, with an area covering 1,170km^2. There are several spectacular waterfalls, including Namtok Cham Pa Thong, and plenty of intriguing rugged rock formations. Get high enough (the highest peak is Don Luang *itself, at 1,426m) and you can find breathtaking views of rolling mountains stretching off into the distance.*

Mae Salong

Mae Salong is a small village, situated 70km north of the city, and accessible through a drive along twisting, scenic mountain roads.

It has a fascinating history: it was settled by a group of Chinese soldiers who fled from the communists in 1949 and, after striking a variety of deals with the Thai government, were allowed to remain. Today it's a quiet village which survives mainly on growing and selling tea. There might not be much to see in the peaceful village itself, but the surroundings are beautiful and well worth exploring.

It's certainly one of Thailand's most unique places, and a rare opportunity to get some kind of authentic experience of China, in an isolated settlement, without visiting the country itself.

Pai

What to Know

Considering how small Pai is – there are only about 30,000 people in the whole district – it draws a surprisingly large number of visitors. It's a very popular choice for budget backpackers. With dozens of spas, meditation retreats and natural wonders to explore, all surrounding the small town of Pai itself, however, there's plenty about for the more moneyed travelers too.

Part of its popularity comes from its proximity to Chiang Mai. It's north west of the big city, close to the Myanmar border, and accessible via a picturesque three hour journey along winding mountain roads (perhaps a little too winding: the journey is notorious for triggering travel sickness, so make sure to take some meds along). It's a natural choice for your next destination when you've finished up in Chiang Mai.

Pai's reputation, at least to a lot of people, is as something of a hippy commune, which isn't really the case. It's true that you'll see a lot of lengthy dreadlocks and vividly colored clothing, on both foreigners and Thais, but these people are in the minority. The place does have an inarguably relaxed feel though, and it has embraced its reputation as a chilled-out oasis, a place to really get away from it all.

As with Chiang Rai, the best parts of Pai are to be found outside the town itself. Rent a scooter (if you don't know how to ride one, there are plenty of people at the rental places who will show you!) and seek out one of the places we've identified, or simply explore at your own speed. Pai is a place where life moves slowly, and where freedom is encouraged in every way. Follow suit with your approach to traveling, at this destination at least.

It's easy to fall under Pai's hypnotic spell, and after arriving you might just end up finding it hard to leave again.

What to See

Walking Street Market

A few of the main roads through Pai are closed to traffic each evening and replaced with stalls. The vendors there sell plenty of potential presents for the people you left back home, as well as clothing (including lots of ponchos, in keeping with the hippy vibe), and lots and lots of food.

We already included a 'What to Eat' section in our Chiang Mai portion of this chapter, but you could effectively write a whole novel about the food available at Pai's Walking Street Market. There are plenty of places selling the normal Thai dishes – Pad Thai, chicken and rice, noodle soup – but, to cater for the disproportionately large number of tourists, there are also offerings from around the world. Pizza, lasagna, sushi, burritos, burgers, Indian food... You name it, and it's probably there; and if it is, it'll definitely be tasty.

Chedi Phra That Mae Yen

The calling card of this particular temple is the large white Buddha statue, which is visible from almost everywhere in Pai. It's only a short walk from the town, although the hundreds of steps up to the top will have you panting for breath.

The Buddha statue is impressive, but the real reason you come here is for the view. It's the most easily accessible viewpoint from town, and when you get up to the top you can see the whole town laid out before you, sunk into a valley of high mountains on either side. Going there just as the sun is setting, and the lights are beginning to flicker on, is an especially memorable experience.

Pai Canyon

A short drive away from the town is Kong Lan, better known to tourists as Pai Canyon. It's not exactly the Grand Canyon, but it's still certainly worth visiting. You can walk along the relatively narrow canyon, peering nervously down at the steep edges, and scramble up red sandstone rocks to access different areas.

It is, of course, also surrounded by mountains covered in tall, green trees in every direction you look. You find these kinds of views everywhere in the north of Thailand, but you never start taking them for granted.

Mo Paeng

Are waterfalls your thing? If so, you've got plenty of choices around Pai. The first one you head to should be Mo Paeng, which is just over 10km west from the town. There are several tiers at the waterfall, and you can swim in the pools to cool off; especially valuable in Thailand's hot season, which even extends to the high altitude in which Pai is set.

Tha Pai Hot Springs

If you've never taken a dip in hot springs before, now's your chance! It's an experience that we'd highly recommend (although not for too long: it is kind of hot in there).

It takes around twenty minutes to get to the Tha Pai Hot Springs. You do have to pay a small entry fee, but that 80 degree goodness will be worth it. On the flipside to taking a dip in the Mo Paeng pools, these hot springs are actually better enjoyed in the chillier weather of the cool season!

6. Southern Thailand: A Slice of Heaven

Having looked at central and northern Thailand, it's time to move downwards towards the region for which the country is arguably most renowned: the south.

There are plenty of spectacular natural wonders and exciting, vibrant urban areas in Thailand, but the south is the place where you might really feel as if you've died and gone to heaven. For lots of people, sunbathing on golden sand, with crystal clear sea water before you, sipping on cocktails is merely a dream. Visit Thailand's south, and you can turn this dream into a reality.

While the rest of Thailand is contained in a large, wide area, the south is more of a long, relatively thin strip of land. Of the three regions we've looked at, the south is by far the least populated, with a total population of only 9 million people. In terms of places to explore, and things to do, however, the south is easily a match for the other two.

There are hundreds of islands in the ocean off both sides of the mainland, falling in the Gulf of Thailand to the east, and alternately the Andaman Sea and the Malacca Strait to the west. To the south there is a land border with Malaysia, but traveling here is highly discouraged due to a long-running, bloody conflict between the two countries in the area.

While the rest of Thailand tends to experience three seasons – hot, rainy and cool – this isn't really the case with the south. While rainfall does increase between May and October, creating a sort of rainy season, the temperature never deviates too far from being, well... really hot! Still, that's exactly what you want from your ideal beach destination!

As is the case in Thailand in general, the more time you have to explore the south, the better for you. With hundreds of islands on offer, however, we thought you'd benefit from having a quick and easy list of three must-visits. In this section we'll be looking at Phuket, Ko Phi Phi and Ko Tao, with mentions of a few of their immediate neighbors.

What to Know

Phuket Province is easily the most densely populated in the south, and the city of Phuket is Thailand's second most popular tourist destination after Bangkok. It takes very little investigation to see why.

Phuket is the largest island in Thailand, measuring a hefty 48km from top to bottom and 21km from side to side, and 600,000 people live there. In short, it's a pretty big place!

Getting there is extremely simple. It's connected by road to the mainland, meaning bus or car journeys are easily made, even from faraway Bangkok. Alternatively, if time is of the essence, you can get a flight to the island's northern airport. Flights from Bangkok may be slightly more than buses, but they're still extremely cheap (normally between $30-40 US).

Considering it's only one island, there's a lot of diversity on Phuket, both in the settlements and in the geography. Phuket Town, in the south east of the island, is the most populated place and is where the administrative buildings are located. It has managed to retain something of a local feel, and has some interesting historical buildings and colonial architecture, but it's certainly not the most popular place with tourists.

That honor would probably go to Patong, which is on the western side of the island. It's certainly the place with the highest volume of things to offer tourists, from hotels, to restaurants, to nightlife. A quieter alternative, not far north of Patong, is Bang Thao. This bay is home to one of the biggest beaches on the island, and, while there are still a fair number of large hotels, it offers a significantly quieter alternative to Patong.

There are several other towns and smaller settlements around the island, each with a slightly different vibe, but hopefully you get the picture already: basically, even though it's only an island and is much smaller than some of the other cities we've looked at, Phuket still has an outstanding amount of variety, and can comfortably offer something for everyone.

Kata Beach

The beaches are really what you came to Phuket for, right?! There are many beaches dotted all around the edges of the island. Some are extremely popular and get quite crowded, especially in high season. Others, like Freedom Beach near Patong, are accessible only via boat, and are therefore very quiet. Kata Beach is a happy medium.

Kata is located on the south west side of the island, and has two beaches. Kata Beach (Kata Yai, if you're asking directions from a local), is a great, safe place to swim. It's not exactly a secret, being visited by a fair number of tourists, but it has still managed to remain relatively unspoiled. You can plonk yourself down into a deckchair, as you can in most Thai beaches, or take cover under the shade of one of the many tall trees along the shore.

If you do find that Kata Yai is a little crowded for your tastes, you'll find its smaller, quieter neighbor Kata Noi nearby.

Bangla Road, Patong

Along with Khao San Road, Patong in Phuket is probably Thailand's most famous party destination, and one of the most famous in all of Southeast Asia.

Bangla Road is the real nightlife hub of Patong, and really of the whole island. It gets very busy almost every night, with the place being rammed with normal bars, go-go bars, cabaret bars... basically every kind of bar you can imagine! There are nightclubs too, if you want to throw some shapes on the dancefloor, including the (in)famous Pinky Bar.

If you want to let off some steam, Bangla Road is the perfect place to do it. The party never really stops, with plenty of people being around throughout the day and some places not closing until sunrise the next morning.

The Surrounding Islands

Phuket Province consists of more than just one island. There are actually a series of smaller islands around the big one – including Coral Island, Racha Island and Maiton Island, which are beautiful and worth visiting in their own right.

Wherever you choose to go, you can't beat the feeling of the wind whipping through your hair as you take a speedboat through the beautiful seawater, while you look forward to arriving shortly at yet another lovely little island.

You can book boat tours from plenty of places around the island, although the most popular place to depart from is Chalong Bay, which is just south of Phuket Town.

FantaSea

The FantaSea entertainment park isn't the most authentic Thai experience, but it does still aim to capture and convey some of the country's culture and heritage in its offerings.

It combines all of your traditional entertainment park favorites – like shops, restaurants and fun fairs – with 'temples' and elephants, to give the whole place a distinctly Thai twist. The centerpiece of the park is the big theater, with its spectacular show featuring acrobats, elephants, and even some local history!

A day trip to FantaSea marks a nice change of place from lazing around on the beaches, which we're assuming you'll spend most of your time doing!

Phang Nga Bay

This comes as close to a 'must-visit' as you'll find in Phuket. If you've ever seen photos of, or visited Halong Bay in Vietnam, picture something close to that.

It's located back towards the mainland, not on the island of Phuket itself, so you'll likely want to commission a boat to take you there. In the vast bay you'll find one of the area's most famous landmarks, James Bond Island (known as Koh Ta Pu, or 'Nail Island', to the locals), where parts of The Man With the Golden Gun were filmed.

Everywhere you look on your boat tour, you'll see tall limestone cliffs stretching away from the mainland or up out of the ocean. You can explore caves, and even a fishing village if you have time. It's a picturesque, gorgeous tour, likely to result in more great holiday snaps than any other trip you undertake from Phuket.

What to Eat

If you thought the food was spicy in the rest of Thailand, just wait until you get to the south. If you're not a fan of that burning-mouth sensation, it's extra-important to make the 'not spicy!' request when you order food.

Just as northern Thai food has been influenced by its proximity to its neighbors – particularly Myanmar – southern Thai food has incorporated elements of cuisine from nearby countries like Malaysia and Indonesia.

Here are a few must-try Thai dishes from the south.

Gaeng

Gaeng is undoubtedly the most famous dish native to southern Thailand. At its roots, it's a spicy curry or soup, with a few different varieties.

Tai pla is probably the most famous Gaeng dish. It tends more towards the 'soup' side of the spectrum, rather than 'curry'. It's primarily made with lots of different fish parts, with pumpkin, eggplant and bamboo shoots thrown in; along with a heck of a lot of spices (the southern Thai trademark).

If you want to try the most unique Gaeng dish in the region, look out for Gaeng Sataw. Its main ingredient is sataw, which means 'stink bean'... Hey, traveling is all about trying new things, remember?!

Khao Yam

This is perhaps the second-most famous southern dish, after Gaeng. To simply look at Khao Yam, you'd think it was a fairly standard rice dish. When you actually tuck in, however, you'll discover a rice saland with a whole mélange of flavors. A wide variety of herbs, some shrimp, and coconut are just some of the ingredients in this complex but tasty dish.

Seafood

In the south, you'll find basically any kind of seafood you can dream of: scallops, lobsters, crabs, squid and plenty more are all present in abundance. The proximity to the sea (really, you can't get any closer than being on a Thai island), lends a phenomenal freshness to the fish. Even if you have the same seafood courses that you ordered in Bangkok or Chiang Mai, the difference in quality of the food will make it seem like a different dish.

Ko Phi Phi

What to Know

Phuket might be the most famous island in Thailand, but Ko Phi Phi is definitely high up the rankings.

It was unfortunately heavily damaged during the tsunami which struck much of Asia in 2004, but great efforts have been made since then to rebuild it, and it's now back to its best. The reconstruction was carried out in a careful way, so that the island's natural beauty was protected; hotels, for example, aren't allowed to be built above a certain height, in order to preserve the views.

Ko Phi Phi is actually a collection of six islands, all part of the Krabi Province, with the main island being Phi Phi Don. Phi Phi Don is the only island in the archipelago which is actually populated, although several of the other islands are frequently visited for their nature and their beaches.

Phi Phi Don is definitely a backpacker hotspot, with lots of parties on offer, but there's also plenty to suit the less boisterous crowd.

What to See

Maya Bay

Maya Bay is the place where 'the beach' from The Beach is located. Well, what else did you expect us to start with?! We already discussed it a little in our '10 Must-See Attractions' chapter, but a visit to Maya Bay is a great thing to tell your friends about when you get home.

You can find Maya Bay on Koh Phi Phi's second biggest island, Phi Phi Leh. It's a short and easy boat ride away from the main island, with a fairly-priced trip easy to book from many places on Phi Phi Don.

The Viewpoint

If you're looking for a postcard-perfect view of Phi Phi Don, this is the place to head to.

Phi Phi Don is basically made up of two islands stuck together by a thin strip of land; you'll find the Viewpoint on the eastern part, slightly north from the conjoined section of the island. It's a bit of a trek, taking around 25-30 minutes to reach the top depending on your fitness and the heat. If you can't make it all the way to the top, don't worry: there are actually three viewpoints in total, with the first being much lower down, and easy to reach, than the third.

The very top is 186m above sea level, and gives you an amazing view of the entire island, and even to the neighboring island of Phi Phi Leh.

Yao Beach

The beach in Maya Bay may actually be the nicest in all of Ko Phi Phi, but unfortunately it's definitely not the most relaxing, with tour boats constantly pulling in and out and scores of DiCaprio fans milling around.

For something that's a little more chilled, and doesn't require a boat ride, head to Yao Beach on Phi Phi Don. It basically offers everything you could want from a beach in Thailand: plenty of space, clean water, great sand, and even the opportunity to go snorkeling in the coral reefs. If you feel like having this slice of heaven on your doorstep, there's plenty of accommodation available right next door!

Monkey Beach

There's not much mystery about this one: you can probably work out its unique selling point from the name. That's right, it's a beach with monkeys!

Monkey Beach (also known as Monkey Bay, or Ao Ling in Thai), is located on the eastern side of the smaller, western part of Phi Phi Don. You can walk to the cove in which it's located or, for a little more adventure, rent a kayak and paddle on over there!

Don't worry about not finding any monkeys when you get there: there are always plenty around, and believe us, they're not afraid of tourists! They'll come right up to you, and even climb on you and take your food; if you've been saving an afternoon snack for an energy boost after a long kayak journey, gobble it up before you get there!

Beach access is completely free. If you're an animal lover, or you're just looking for something absolutely unique, a visit to Monkey Beach is not to be missed!

Ko Tao

What to Know

Phuket and Ko Phi Phi do have some similarities, particularly in the volume of nightlife on offer, which tends to attract visitors who are looking, to some degree, to party. Ko Tao is a very different kind of place.

There has always been a degree of nightlife on Ko Tao, but in recent years the place seems to have mellowed and become calmer. Even as it has become a more popular destination over the years, as Thailand's tourism trade in general has exploded, it's still retained something of a small island feel. Its actual physical size aids this; Ko Tao measures in at only 21km²; a fraction of the size of Phuket, at 576km².

By far the island's main attraction is diving, which should give you some clue as to how great the water is which surrounds Ko Tao. In general Ko Tao is an active place, with plenty of physical and fun activities on offer, including hiking and rock climbing.

Don't worry, though. If you're looking for a more classic Thai island experience, Ko Tao still has plenty of beaches to offer, especially considering its relatively small size.

It's also worth noting that the ebbs and flows of tourism work slightly differently here. Thailand's generally-accepted high season is from December until February, with another mini boost in July and August. In Ko Tao, however, that mini boost basically becomes a second high season. Southern Thailand in general becomes busier during this period, with the rain beginning to fall more heavily in the middle and north of the country, but with Ko Tao being so famous for its diving – a popular activity with tourists – this second high season is especially prevalent there.

One final fun fact before we get onto the next section: Ko Tao means 'Turtle Island'. Nice!

A Diving Instructor!

Seriously; if you want to learn how to dive, properly, Ko Tao is the place for you. A whopping 7,000 people learn to do it here every year, making it easily the most popular place for newbie divers in Thailand.

Considering the relative smallness of the island, there are a vast array of diving instruction schools (reportedly as many as 46), for both scuba diving and free diving, who'll be happy to teach you in exchange for a few thousand baht. After a few fun lessons, you'll be fully qualified to dive whenever you please. Of course, even though there are plenty of options out there, make sure to pick the one that best suits you. Do your research online beforehand to make sure you're getting an instructor who knows their stuff, tells you what you need to know, and offers fair value for money.

If you're already an experienced diver, you'll find Ko Tao's conditions are perfect for you. The water is pleasantly warm, the visibility is good, and there's an aquarium's-worth of underwater animals for you to observe, including reef sharks, stingrays, turtles, and lots and lots of fish.

Ao Leuk Bay

Between the costs, putting on all the equipment, and so on, we can see why diving isn't for everybody. Fear not, though; even in the diving capital of Thailand, there's still something on offer for you!

Snorkeling is a great alternative to diving, allowing you to get stuck in to that beautiful blue water, without the hassle or expense of diving. The best place on Ko Tao to do a bit of snorkeling is almost certainly Ao Leuk Bay.

Ao Leuk is located on the southeast side of the island, not far from Shark Island (not as scary as it sounds; we're sorry to disappoint you, but its name comes from its resemblance to a shark fin, not because it's Jaws's favorite holiday hangout). It's easy to reach on foot, or by bike. The beach is nice enough to chill on, but with rocks so close to the shore, and the presence of a nice cross-section of aquatic wildlife, the water is the perfect place to go snorkeling.

If you want to go a little further out, head northwards to nearby Ao Leuk Point, which also features calm water conditions which are excellent for snorkeling.

Mae Haad Village

If you're tired out from a day of diving (or snorkeling), and/or recovering from a hangover, head to Mae Haad. It's the hub of the island, with enough bars and restaurants to satisfy the tastes of every visitor.

Mae Haad is also the main entry and departure point to the island. With plenty of accommodation available, that also makes it a very convenient place to base yourself. The concentration of helpful services there, including ticket offices, internet cafes (that's right; they're still a thing!) and banks, only adds to its usefulness.

Sairee Beach

Technically, Mae Haad does have a beach of its own, but you're better heading to Sairee Beach, which is slightly nicer and only a short walk away.

It's the largest beach on the island, meaning you should have ample space in which to spread out your towels and build your sandcastles. If you're looking to party in the evening, Sairee should definitely be your destination of choice. There are bars and restaurants all along the beach where you can grab a drink, but don't worry; they don't spoil the beauty and peacefulness of the beach itself.

Ko Nang Yuan

If you didn't get the picture already, Ko Tao is a pretty nice place. It's a natural inclination when you visit the south of Thailand though, that when you're on one island you'll want to explore the other islands that surround it!

If this feeling takes you while you're on Ko Tao, head over to Ko Nang Yuan. It sits just off the northwest side of Ko Tao, and it's easy to reach by a small boat taxi or a larger ferry.

Considering how small it is, there's a surprising amount to do on Ko Nang Yuan. It's actually made up of three separate small islands, which are all connected by thin strips of sand, so you can easily walk between them. It has the diving opportunities that you'd expect from the area, and great places to go snorkeling too, including the stunning Japanese Garden on the eastern side.

There is also, of course, also a picture-perfect beach. If you're still not bored of those by this point, take yet another opportunity to spend a relaxing few hours soaking up some rays!

As we mentioned in the introductory first chapter, Thailand's economy has come on leaps and bounds in the past few decades. Amongst a raft of other improvements, the country's transport infrastructure has also seen massive developments. These have primarily been fantastic for Thai people, of course... but they've been pretty great for tourists too!

In fact, in most cases you won't see much of a difference between Thailand's travel systems, and those to be found in some of the richest countries in the world, like the USA. Planes, cars, buses, trains and boats are all viable methods of transport, and will all take you exactly where you want to go cheaply and reliably.

Let's take a deeper look into how you can get around the tremendous country of Thailand.

Bangkok is home to the country's two largest airports, both of which fly a huge volume of international flights. The chances are that your trip to Thailand will begin at one of these.

Suvarnabhumi was only opened for international flights in 2006, but is far and away the busiest airport in the country. In fact, it's the twentieth busiest airport in the whole world. Don Mueang is the second busiest airport in Thailand, and has been open for commercial flights since 1924, making it the one of the oldest airports in the world.

Phuket Airport provides the quickest entry into Thailand's south. Frequent flights are available there from nearby countries like Malaysia and Singapore, and of course from other airports around Thailand.

Chiang Mai is the country's fourth busiest airport, and provides an easy gateway to the north (especially because of its proximity to the rest of the city).

There are plenty of other, smaller airports dotted around the country too, useful mostly for domestic flights. Just some of the other places to house airports include **Krabi, Udon Thani and Samui.**

As you can see, Thailand is extremely well-serviced by air. Fares both inside Thailand, and to nearby countries, are cheap, even if you book them at short notice, and obviously provide the quickest way to get around.

Thailand's roads have a reputation as being dangerous, mostly due to alarming statistics on road casualties which pick up a lot of attention from international media. These reports are extremely misleading though.

Firstly, 70% of the accidents take place on motorbikes. If you're particularly worried about getting into an accident, just stay on four wheels instead of two. Secondly, a huge proportion of the accidents occur because of the Thai people's widespread (and somewhat baffling), disregard for basic safety measures... like wearing a seatbelt. Follow some common sense and buckle up and, just like you're taught in school, you'll immediately be a lot safer.

*When you're actually on the ground, you can see for yourself that the Thais are generally excellent drivers. At first glance the roads may seem chaotic, with motorbikes weaving in and out of cars, and trucks piled to the brim with either goods or people. When you actually get behind the wheel of a car, however, you'll find that driving, whether it be out in the country or in a busy city, is absolutely fine. Because of this, and because of the additional freedom you gain to explore at your own pace, you should definitely consider **hiring a car**.*

*If that's not for you, don't worry; you can get **buses** pretty much anywhere you want to go. Shorter hops are usually made in minibuses, which are cheap and move quickly, but aren't always necessary the comfiest places to be. Longer hauls, by contrast, are almost always made on huge, multistoried coaches. These tend to be very comfortable indeed, with their large, cozy reclining seats. If you're looking to save money on accommodation, take a night bus to your next destination. They're quiet and comfy, giving you a good chance at a decent night's sleep, and they'll save you from booking into a hotel for a night.*

*When it comes to bus services inside the actual cities, however, Thailand is lacking. **Chiang Mai** effectively has no bus service at all (there's just one that goes round and round the ring road), so you're completely reliant on the ubiquitous songthaews; red, public taxis that basically look like pickup trucks. Likewise, **Phuket** has minimal public transport available. The most notable service on offer is one that leaves from Phuket Town (Ranong Road, specifically, in the Old Town), and takes you across the island to the various beaches. It's useful, but not at all comfortable.*

Bangkok has by far the best bus services. Just walk down a main road for five minutes and you'll likely be passed by at least ten buses (all of which seem to have particularly loud engines). Fares depend on which service you use, but they're always cheap (under 50 baht). The seats are fairly comfortable, and the buses are either air-conditioned, or have all their windows open.

However – and we can't stress this clearly enough – make sure you know exactly where your bus stop is, which service you need, and where you're getting off, before you leave your hotel room. The bus stops almost never have writing in English, or maps. Use Google Maps to plan your journey, and it'll tell you exactly which number bus you need to look out for. Once aboard, it's useful to have a screenshot or a web page open on your phone, showing your destination in written Thai. You can then show that to the conductor, when they come to collect your fare, and they should help you get off at the right stop.

Keeping in mind what we said earlier about road safety, you could also consider hiring a **motorbike**. If you're comfortable driving one, they really are the perfect way to explore a local area, and make day trips to wherever you want to go at your own pace. Basically every place in Thailand will have a wide selection of rental shops. You can take the bikes out for a day, or longer if you'd prefer, for a minimal sum of money. Gas is also very cheap, so keeping them running certainly won't break the bank.

Despite linking most of the country together, and having a network that connects across the country to all major destinations, trains are a curiously unpopular method of transport with travelers, especially compared to buses.

On the one hand, this could simply be because the buses in Thailand, for longer journeys especially, are so comfortable, convenient and reasonably priced. With such a good service available by road, there isn't much need to look elsewhere.

The train system itself does have its drawbacks. Train travel in Thailand is slower than going via bus. You may look at timetables online and think that the journey durations look roughly the same, but this is misleading: there's a running joke that the trains run on 'Thai time', meaning that they usually arrive an hour late, at the very least. Train tickets also tend to cost more than bus tickets, especially when it's a sleeper train and you start adding things like a charge for having air-con.

So, are we saying you should avoid Thai trains at all costs? Absolutely not!

Firstly, traveling by rail is more pleasant than traveling by road; it just is. You have the gentle, soothing rocking of the train as it moves over the tracks. You get much nicer views, particularly in Thailand, where on your car journeys through the middle of the country you'll only really see the unending shops and restaurants lining the roads.

Secondly, it helps you to dodge traffic. Thailand's main roads don't really go around cities and towns, as they do in lots of countries; they go straight through the middle, which can often result in being stuck in traffic. As well as the inherent frustration of being forced to sit still, this can actually lead to buses sometimes taking longer than trains to arrive at their destination. This advantage is especially pronounced on shorter journeys, where the road route doesn't ever really depart from heavily populated (and congested) areas. The road from Bangkok to Ayutthaya, for example, is short but very busy. A train will whisk you right there.

Bangkok is the only city in Thailand to have its own internal train system, and it really is an excellent system.

There are four lines in total – two over-ground, and two underground – which crisscross much of the main part of the city. The service is reliable, clean, efficient, easy to use, and fast. In a city like Bangkok, where the traffic can often by crippling, this is incredibly useful. There's also the Airport Rail Link, which connects from the city center all the way out to Suvarnabhumi Airport: a great choice if you don't want the volume of traffic determining whether or not you catch your flight!

With everything north of Bangkok being landlocked, this section obviously only applies to those parts of the country which run from the capital southwards.

In Bangkok, you'll quickly learn that the number one rule of getting around the city quickly is to avoid the roads at all costs. Traffic jams don't even seem to occur at specific times, or because of particular events; they're simply always there.

Whilst the Skytrain and Metro services don't extend far enough to the west to encompass the old town and its surrounding area, there is still a viable alternative to buses and taxis. Boats run frequently throughout the day along the Chao Phraya river (from north to south), and the Khlong Saen Saep canal (from east to west).

There are plenty of stops on both routes, and although they won't drop you exactly where you want to go, as a taxi might, there's a high chance you'll reach your final destination faster, even if you have to walk a little bit. The prices are certainly more favorable, with ticket fares beginning at only 10 baht.

Practicality aside, it makes a refreshing change to be out on the water in a city like Bangkok, where you almost always find yourself on bustling pavements and roads!

When it comes to the south of Thailand, the fact that Phuket is the only island accessible by road means boats aren't simply an option any more; they're a necessity.

Unfortunately for you – and because the vast majority of people who use them are tourists, not locals – this means that boat companies can basically charge whatever prices they want. A journey from Phuket to nearby Ko Phi Phi will likely cost you 300-400 baht. The boats also move pretty slowly: that same journey, however close it might look on the map, will likely take 2 or 3 hours.

Still, there are worse places to be for 3 hours than crossing the Andaman Sea, in perfect weather conditions, on your way to visit another amazing Thai island!

As you'll quickly learn, the Thais love any excuse to have a good party! Their parties can be based around religious festivals, birthdays, or even events from vastly different cultures like Christmas.

Whatever the occasion, they go to a great deal of planning in the buildup, ensuring everything is meticulously scheduled and arranged. They work extremely hard on making each event as memorable and visually special as possible, from intricate flower arrangements to highly choreographed dances. The food is, of course, plentiful and delicious, whatever the occasion.

Here we'll be taking a look at some of the most important (and fun!) festivals to take place throughout the year, broken down by month. If your schedule will allow it, it's a great idea to plan your holiday to align with one of these events, for an even more memorable visit than you would otherwise have.

(Note: dates for many of these festivals vary from year to year; these are the probable dates for 2017)

January

1st - New Year's Day

Thai people may celebrate their own new year in April, with the Songkran Festival (which is one of the best events on the calendar; more on that later!), but they still use a western calendar which flips over on January 1st.

They take an extended, four day holiday for the occasion, and celebrate in much the same way as the western world: with a countdown to the moment itself, and with a big party!

If you're looking for a big party yourself, head to Bangkok: its already-bouncing nightlife only becomes more fun on New Year's Eve, making it one of the world's best places to celebrate.

28th - Chinese New Year

Ethnically speaking Thailand is pretty diverse, and there's a significant Chinese population in the country. In the buildup to the big day you'll start seeing 'Happy Chinese New Year!' banners everywhere you look, particularly in the big cities. If you want to celebrate the event in style, the best place to go is Bangkok's extensive Chinatown.

February

14th – Valentine's Day

As it is in much of the world, the 14th is a day to celebrate your love for a special someone. The Thais are normally reserved in their public displays of affection with each other, but they loosen the rules a little on this day.

For your touristic purposes, we can't imagine a better place to spend Valentine's Day with your special someone than on an idyllic, secluded beach in the south of Thailand. If you're stuck in a city, don't worry: plenty of the restaurants and bars offer Valentine's Day promotions to ensure you still have a romantic night to remember.

March

17th – National Muay Thai Day

March is actually a very quiet month for festivals in Thailand, perhaps because everyone's already gearing up for the big one in April, Songkran.

National Muay Thai Day isn't big enough to warrant a national holiday, but it's still a perfect time to check out Thailand's national sport in person if you haven't been already. Events are held at gyms and arenas around the country, with Ayutthaya – the home of legendary fighter Nai Khanom Tom – being the top place to be.

April

6th – Chakri Day

The Thai people love their royal family, and this public holiday gives them an opportunity to pay their respects. On the 6th, the people commemorate the beginning of the Chakri Dynasty, which is still in power today.

13th – 15th – Songkran Festival

This is the big one!

Songkran Festival – perhaps better known to foreigners as the 'Water Festival' – is a three day extravaganza celebrating the beginning of a new Thai year. It's celebrated by Thai people all around the world, but nowhere near the extent to which it's celebrated in the homeland.

It's basically a three day extravaganza, but the highlight is, of course, the water. The Thai people throw water over Buddha statues to symbolize purification... then start throwing it all over each other!

It if matches up with your dates at all, you should really try to be in Thailand for Songkran; you'll be in for an experience that you'll definitely never forget! Just make sure to bring a towel along.

May

10th – Visakha Bucha

Whilst nowhere near as fun as Songkran, Visakha Bucha is still a big day in the Thai calendar. This religious festival is perhaps the most important religious commemoration of all.

The aim is to mark the three biggest events in the Buddha's life: his birth, his reaching of enlightenment, and his death and ascent to nirvana. Temples around the country are packed on the day of Visakha Bucha with Thais recognizing these landmarks.

June

(Date varies) – Hua Hin Jazz Festival

June is another quiet month for celebrations in the Thai calendar. If you're in Thailand and you want to celebrate something though, head to the coastal city of Hua Hin! It's an easy journey from Bangkok, and you can pass a nice day and night listening to some of the finest jazz musicians in Thailand, as well as some international guests.

July

9th – Khao Phansa

Khao Pansa is another important religious festival (we'll warn you now; alcohol is banned on this day!), marking the beginning of the three-month long Buddhist lent. The monks will be restricted to one particular temple for the whole period, so Thais take their chance to make various offering to the monks, including candles (because historically monks could only light their temples with candles during the lent period) and clothes.

August

12th – The Queen's Birthday

The birthday of the Thai queen (currently Queen Sirikit, wife of the late King Bhumibol Adulyadej), also doubles as Mother's Day in Thailand. Thai people pass a long, four-day weekend, spending most of their time with their families, and with children honoring their own mothers.

September

5th – Chinese Hungry Ghost Festival

(Note: the dates for this do vary, although it usually falls in late August or early September)

The Chinese Hungry Ghost Festival represents another example of Thailand's multicultural approach to festivities.

This occasion marks the day on which (according to Chinese mythology, anyway) the gates of hell are opened, and hungry spirits are allowed to roam the earth. People make various offerings to their ancestors, including food... as you might expect.

Although Thai people do celebrate it to an extent, it is primarily a Chinese festivals, so you'll want to head to somewhere like Chinatown in Bangkok for the full experience.

October

5th — Awk Phansa

At long last the three-month Buddhist lent is over, and the monks are finally released from their temples. The Thai people celebrate the monks' feat by visiting temples and providing plenty of offerings, including food and clothing. They also celebrate by... having boat races! We told you the Thai people always find a way to have fun.

9th — Vegetarian Festival

We think this will definitely interest a certain subset of foodies out there!

At the heart of the Vegetarian Festival, which lasts for over a week, is the idea of abstinence, and the opportunity for Thai people to cleanse their bodies and minds. They avoid meat, fish and dairy products, ideally for nine days and nine nights.

The Vegetarian Festival happens all around Thailand, although it's most prominently observed in Phuket. Here it's a full, colorful festivity, with some 'interesting' wrinkles. Chief amongst these is people practicing various harmful procedures on themselves, including body-piercing and fire-walking, with the belief that the Chinese gods will protect them from harm if they are pure. It's definitely worth checking out, although not if you're at all squeamish!

4ᵗʰ – Loy Krathong/ Yi Peng

This is another one of the most internationally-known celebrations on the Thai calendar, probably second only to Songkran in its fame.

Also known as the Festival of Light, Loy Krathong is the festival where little rafts are created and filled with flowers and a candle. People light the candles and make a wish, then place the rafts on lakes, rivers and ponds, with the idea being that the person's sins will be washed away.

In northern Thailand this is also combined with Yi Peng, known as the Lantern Festival. You've likely seen photos already of this; it's the festival where people light candles in a paper lantern, which fills with hot air until it flies away. The symbolism behind it is that the lantern represents a release of bad memories and a movement towards the future, and it also pays respect to the Buddha.

Being in Chiang Mai during Yi Peng, and watching hundreds of orange lanterns float away into the dark night sky as the crowds below look up in wonder, is an incredible experience which you're never likely to forget. If you possibly can, aim to time your holiday in Thailand to coincide with this.

December

25th – Christmas Day (obviously!)

That's right: even though 95% of the Thai population is Buddhist, they still celebrate Christmas!

It may not be a public holiday, but it's still a big celebration. Shopping malls are covered in decorations, just as they are in western countries, except the decorations here have that certain degree of class and creativity which the Thais seem to bring to all their design work. Likewise, restaurants and bars offer plenty of special celebratory deals for your Christmas lunch. Thai people themselves often give and receive gifts to mark the occasion.

If you want to spend your Christmas Day in beautiful, warm weather, with clear blue skies, head to Thailand; we can think of worse places to celebrate.

Let's get this out of the way immediately: Thailand is not a particularly dangerous country to visit.

Since mid-2014 the US government hasn't issued a single Travel Warning or Travel Alert for Thailand. It was the victim of a few bombings, in 2015 and 2016, which you may have read about in the news. These seemed to be isolated incidents, though, and unfortunately it doesn't differ from most places in the world in terms of a background threat of terrorism. For the most part, and particularly in the places you're likely to visit, the chances are massively in your favor that you won't encounter any problems at all.

Staying safe in Thailand is generally no different from staying safe in much of the world. The same common sense rules and basic logic apply; i.e. don't wander down dark alleyways late at night, don't leave your drink unattended when you're in a bar or a club, don't leave valuables in your hotel room if you can help it, and so on.

That being said, there are still a number of Thai-specific rules of safety which you should observe, to have the most trouble-free visit you possibly can. We'll look at a few areas of safety now, including places you shouldn't visit, scams to watch out for, the situation on the roads and a little look into the wildlife.

Places

You can go almost anywhere in the country, without any increased threat of danger to your person.

The only truly dangerous place in Thailand is the most southern part, near the land border with Malaysia. There has been a conflict there since 1948, which is ongoing to this day. Violence and fatalities occur on an extremely frequent basis. Please note, however that we are only talking about the areas right next to the border here: the violence has not spread to anywhere near the tourist destinations in the south, such as Phuket or Ko Phi Phi.

Unless it's absolutely central, we would advise not going to the southernmost part of Thailand. If you'd like to move on from Thailand to Malaysia, cheap flights are available from Phuket and Bangkok.

Also note that extreme caution should be observed right on the borders with Cambodia and Laos, because of a significant number of mines and unexploded munitions from previous wars. These are not an active threat at all to you if you stick to the usual tourist areas, and built-up settlements; just don't stray too far from the roads and well-worn paths, and you'll be fine!

These border areas also carry a significant risk of dengue fever and malaria from mosquitos. Again, though, this is easily combated by covering up with clothing, wearing spray, or – to combat malaria, at least – even taking anti-malaria pills. Follow these basic, sensible precautions and you won't have anything to worry about.

Theft

We already mentioned that most basic piece of advice; don't leave too many valuables in your room if you can help it. Hotel room theft isn't any more prevalent in Thailand than it is elsewhere in the world, but it's still a sensible habit to get into. The same goes for pickpocketing: it's not an especially big problem in Thailand, but you should zip up those pockets, or at least keep your hands in them, when you're out in a big crowd.

A more common problem is robbery on the street. There are regular incidents with tourists where a local will snatch an expensive piece of jewelry the tourist is wearing, or perhaps a handbag, then run to a motorcycle where another local is waiting, before they both escape at high speed. The most basic precaution to take is to simply leave that expensive jewelry at home. If you must bring it, keep it out of sight when you're walking around. Try to keep your valuables in something a little harder to snatch than a handbag too, like a backpack. You might lose a few style points, but it's a lot better than the alternative!

Incidents with Locals

We touched on this earlier, but it's best to avoid getting into any kind of conflict with a local if you can help it. If the police get involved, they almost certainly won't take your side, and the language barrier definitely won't help the situation.

We're sure we don't have to even mention this to you good folk, but never, ever get a fight with a local. They may often look slight, but when five or ten of their friends get involved, this won't really matter. Even if you've had a few drinks, and you're high on life, just keep those fists tucked away!

The Thai people are notoriously welcoming and friendly, and in the more popular touristic areas they have plenty of experience of foreigners, so this is highly unlikely to be an issue anyway.

Wildlife

Thailand has a diverse range of wildlife which you might not find back home; at least, not in the wild.

Most of these animals are completely harmless, but in the wrong circumstances they can be dangerous. The number one danger, as you can probably guess, is rabies. You want to avoid being bitten at all costs, which means that, however cute and fluffy the animals seem, you should avoid feeding or petting them, just in case.

The dogs that stroll around seemingly all of Thailand, for example, are almost always placid. They're also almost always unclean, however, so don't get too close. If one does seem as if it's getting aggressive, simply try to stay calm and walk away slowly; don't run, whatever you do, or the dog might give chase. In the worst case scenario, if you do get bitten, head to a hospital immediately.

It's generally the same story with monkeys. You'll find monkeys at spots around Thailand; on Monkey Beach in Ko Phi Phi, for example. The monkeys in these spots are very accustomed to tourists, and shouldn't cause any trouble. If food becomes involved, though, they can turn aggressive. Enjoy yourself, but stay alert!

Drinking Water

Whatever you do, however thirsty you get, do not drink the tap water in Thailand! It's certainly not the worst tap water in the world, but in a lot of the country it still doesn't meet international health standards.

It's also very cheap and easy to get good, safe drinking water in Thailand, so this shouldn't really be an issue. You can get big 1.5L bottles of water for around 14 baht ($0.4 US). If you're on a tight budget, you can even refill these bottles at one of the refilling stations which are dotted around the bigger cities, for a measly 1 baht.

Drugs

It's a pretty universal rule when traveling that you shouldn't accept drugs from a stranger, wherever you are.

Partly this is because you have no idea what it is; every year there are tragic stories of travelers dying from falsely-sold, harmful substances, in lots of different countries.

The other reason, of course, is the legality. In Thailand, drugs are very, very illegal! The police won't care whether you're foreign or not; they'll chuck you in jail just as they would a local person. If you're discovered with something like marijuana you're less likely to face actual jail time, but the policeperson will demand a hefty payment, usually climbing into thousands of baht.

Is it really worth the risk, when there's so much drug-free fun out there to be had in Thailand?!

Roads

For a detailed description of the road safety issues in Thailand, head to our 'Getting Around Thailand' chapter. If you're too lazy, here's a quick summary!

Thailand has an international reputation of having extremely dangerous roads, but this has very little to do with foreigners. If you take the same basic safety precautions as you would at home, like wearing a seatbelt, and not driving after you've been drinking, you'll hopefully be fine.

Note that the Thais drive on the left-hand side of the road. If you're used to driving on the right, make sure to take it easy when it's your first time behind the wheel, or on a bike, to acclimatize.

Prostitution

Technically prostitution is illegal in Thailand... but you wouldn't know it from being there.

Thailand has a reputation of being – amongst many other, more innocent things! – a destination for sex tourists. Estimates vary, but most studies agree that there are a whopping 150,000-200,000 sex workers currently operating in the country. It's also estimated that an incredible $6.4 billion each year is spent on sex workers, accounting for 10% of Thailand's GDP. Numbers aside, a simple walk around certain areas of Bangkok or Pattaya will easily confirm just how widespread it is!

If this is one of your reasons for going to Thailand, then rest assured that you probably won't get in legal trouble for engaging the services of one of these workers; for one reason or another, police turn a blind eye to the trade. Do, however, remember your sex education lessons from high school: HIV/Aids is very prevalent in the sex trade across Thailand, so please take all the necessary precautions.

Scams

As with every major destination, scams for tourists are widespread in Thailand. A lot of them are localized, so make sure to do some in-depth research on any new location you go to in preparation. Others, however, are commonly found around the country.

One that's common in Thailand, and much of Southeast Asia, is found at markets. If there's not a price already written for something on the stall, be prepared to be charged double what a local person would have to pay for it. Unless you befriend (or marry) a Thai person, and bring them with you, you're just going to have to take the hit on this. Luckily for you, Thailand is such a relatively cheap country that it still shouldn't make too much of a hole in your wallet!

Another way to cut down on your scamming costs is to never buy a tour, a day trip, or anything like that, from a seller on the street. They'll almost always charge vastly over-

inflated prices. It's much cheaper to simply go straight to one of the many, many tour agencies in any major tourist destination.

You'll find another common scam with drivers of taxis and tuk-tuks. You'll ask them to take you to a popular destination – the Grand Palace, for example. They'll say OK, and start driving, only to stop at a seemingly random clothes shop or café. As you can probably guess, it won't be random at all – it'll be owned by them, or a family member – and you'll have to stop there for ten minutes to browse the wares before carrying on. Whenever you give a destination to a driver, clarify that you want to go straight there! If they even mention a stop on the way, or start to slow down clearly before you've reached your destination, give them a firm 'No!'. Most of the drivers are very friendly, and have ferried around plenty of tourists, so they should be fine with this.

Finally comes a scam that's easy to fall for, because it concerns monks! Of course, they won't usually be real monks, but with their shaved heads and orange robes, how are you to know better? These fake monks will come up to you and ask for donations; something that a normal monk would never do, with alms giving finishing at 8am. It may feel bad, because... they look just like monks, but if you really want to make a donation, go directly to a temple and do it there.

In Case of Emergency

Just in case anything bad does happen, the emergency number in Thailand is 191. Even if you haven't bought a Thai visa for your phone, don't worry; your mobile should automatically use whatever networks it can find to connect the call.

If anything really bad happens, like losing your passport or becoming embroiled in legal troubles, visit or otherwise contact your country's embassy as quickly as possible for help.

Of Thailand's many, many attractive features, which help to draw millions upon millions of visitors to its shores each year, it has to be said that one of the most attractive of all is the visa situation! It's flexible, cheap, and easy to navigate.

In this chapter we'll take a look at the various types of visas you can get, for both shorter and longer stays, how to extend your visas or get new ones, and what to do in the event of overstaying your visa.

Ah, Thailand's glorious visa exemption, friend to backpackers and other budget travelers from around the world. This is, of course, because it's completely free!

Unfortunately the visa exemption isn't open to everyone, but it is available to residents of over fifty different countries. Make sure you check whether or not your country is on the list by heading to the Thai Embassy website (ThaiEmbassy.com).

The visa exemption isn't a magical waiver, however, to live out all your Thai dreams. There are some rules and stipulations to take into account:

- *The amount of time you're allowed to stay in Thailand depends on which country you're from. Most countries have up to 30 days in the kingdom, but a few lucky countries – like Argentina and Brazil – get a whopping 90 days... for free!*
- *The amount of time you're given depends on whether you enter by air or by land. By air you'll be allowed the full amount of time (30 or 90 days). By land, however, you might see this reduced to 15 days depending on where you're from.*
- *Your visit has to be purely for tourism purposes. No working of any kind is permitted.*
- *In the past – and you may have read about this online already – people could go on 'visa runs'. This meant that when their visa exemptions ran out they could simply hop over the border – to Cambodia, Laos, etc. – then come right back in again and get a brand new visa exemption. This is no longer the case. After your visa exemption period expires you must properly leave the country, and if you want to re-enter you have to get an actual visa. This means going to a Thai embassy in one of the neighboring countries, filling in the paperwork, and paying the fee.*
- *If you're entering by land, you can only have two visa exemptions in a calendar year. If you're coming in by air, you can have as many as you like. You might start to be questioned by border police, however, if you rack up six exemptions in a calendar year.*
- *If you read the official guidelines, on the website for your local Thai embassy or on ThaiEmbassy.com, you might see the requirement such as 'must provide proof of online travel'. In actuality, you almost certainly won't need this: border officials have been turning a blind eye to it for years. If you want to be absolutely sure,*

however, just buy the cheapest flight you can from a budget airline, even if you have no intention of using it: you should be able to get something for $30 US, or cheaper.

- ***Important note***: *the rules on visas for Thailand, and especially for visa exemptions, change all the time. They can change multiple times in the same calendar year. Make sure you check the rules for your specific country, in detail, along with all the latest updates from border control, before visiting.*

Longer-term Visas

Visa exemptions are a great, free way to enjoy a month's holiday in Thailand (or three months, if you're lucky enough to enjoy 90-day exemptions!). If you can spare the time, however, you should certainly look towards a longer stay in the country, to explore everything you can. Thirty days gives you time to check out the main sights and spots, along with a smattering of off-the-beaten-track destinations. With two or three months at your disposal, however, you'll be able to take your time, and travel more slowly.

To get a proper Tourist Visa, you'll need to visit your local Thai embassy or consulate in your own country, fill in a formal application form, and usually make a payment.

There are two main types of tourist visa: single entry, and multiple entry. As the name suggests, single entry visas only allow you to enter the country once: if you leave, you won't be allowed to come back on the same visa. Multiple entry visas allow you to leave and come back again.

So, why doesn't everybody just get a multiple entry visa? Well, for starters, they are much more expensive. At the time of writing, a single entry visa costs $40 US, whereas a multiple entry visa costs substantially more at $200. They're also more difficult to get. For a single entry, you basically just fill in a couple of forms and you're done. As an example of how much more difficult it is to get a multiple entry, they require you to show your bank accounts, for the past six months, with each statement displaying a balance of $7,000 US.

Is it really worth the extra cost and hassle of getting a multiple entry visa instead of a single entry? The answer is, of course, up to you (but we'd say 'no'!).

Visa Extensions

A tourist visa will grant you a stay in Thailand for up to 60 days; twice as long as the standard visa exemption. Your time isn't necessarily limited to that, however. If you still don't feel like you want to leave as the 60-day mark approaches, it's a pretty painless process to get an extension. You can also extend your visa exemption for 30 days.

There are places to extend your visa in all the normal major cities you'd expect, like Bangkok, Pattaya, Chiang Mai and Phuket. Bring a couple of passport-sized photos with you, your passport itself, and some cash (1,900 baht at the time of writing). At the office itself you'll have to fill in a couple of forms (including an address for where you're staying – make sure you bring this with you!) and wait for a bit before sitting down with an immigration official. They'll look over your forms and, all being well, take your money and give you a whole new thirty days in their country!

In a country where time doesn't always seem to be of the essence, and life generally moves slowly, the immigration offices actually tend to be pretty speedy. You can be in and out, with a brand new extension, within an hour. You should still aim to get there as early in the morning as possible, though, just to be sure.

Overstay

We all miss deadlines every now and again; it happens to the best of us! Or, perhaps, you've already extended your visa and you still want to stay a little bit longer. The good news is that Thailand is a pretty forgiving country when it comes to overstaying your visa.

That being said, overstaying your visa is technically illegal. If you're unlucky enough to be stopped and searched by an immigration official, or you get involved in an altercation with the police, and the authorities find out you've overstayed your visa, you'll almost certainly be jailed.

If, when you come to leave the country, you've only overstayed your visa by one day, it will usually be overlooked. If it's any longer, however, you'll incur a charge of 500 baht (around $14 US) for each day you've overstayed your visa. This fine runs up to a maximum amount of 20,000 baht (which equates to a 40 day overstay).

If you only overstay by a few days, you'll likely be able to simply pay your fine and fill in a couple of forms before being sent on your way. For longer violations, however, the penalties are more serious. From 90 days of overstaying onwards, you'll be banned from re-entering Thailand for a certain amount of time. If you overstay by 90 days, you'll be banned for 1 year; if you overstay by a year, you'll be banned for 3 years; and so on.

Repeated overstays lead to more severe punishments, as you would expect. If you overstay several times you'll get a stamp in your passport which basically says that you don't respect immigration laws; obviously this could be a problem when you look to travel to other countries. Eventually, if you push it too far, you can be banned for life from Thailand.

Thailand is a country where it's very, very easy to lose track of the date. Just do your best to keep your departure date in mind, plan your trip as best as you can so that you see everything you want in your allotted time, and this won't even be a problem. Again, even if you do end up overstaying by a few days, by accident or by choice, it almost certainly won't have any significant consequences.

11. Time to Book Your Flights

We're drawing towards the end of this particular literary trip around Thailand.

We started off with a view from 30,000ft, looking at Thailand's situation on a macro level, in terms of its economy, its history, and how it came to be what it is today. We zoomed in a little closer, to look at what really makes Thailand... Thailand; its people, and their culture and customs. We moved closer still, to look at the surefire can't-miss things that should be included on the itinerary of any Thai trip, like the Grand Palace and the beach from The Beach. Eventually we got right down to ground level, and looked in more detail at some of the locations you're sure to visit if you have the time, and what you should do there.

We also looked at some practical information which should be valuable to you, especially regarding the safety tips. As a final note on that subject, we want to stress something to you in the immortal words of The Hitchhiker's Guide to the Galaxy: whatever happens, don't panic!

However exotic and far away it may seem to you, remember that Thailand is a major tourist destination, and has been for many years now. Wherever you're going in the country, there's plenty of information available to you, down to the nicest restaurant, near to you, that's in your price range.

If you're the kind of person who doesn't like to freewheel their traveling (which is completely fine!), just do your research before you go anywhere new. Even if you're out and about, without access to internet or a guidebook, and even if you don't speak a word of Thai, you'll find someone to help you. Ask a policeperson, or a waitress in a restaurant, or a hostel owner. They'll almost certainly be willing to help you, or they'll find someone who can.

We wanted to give you some of the most important safety tips for your Thailand visit, but if you keep these in mind, and follow basic rules of etiquette, logic and common sense, you really don't have anything to worry about.

Before we go, we have a few closing thoughts. Thailand is pretty much the perfect travel destination, and we want to explain why.

Why do we travel, especially so far from our own homes?

Is a lot of it to do with getting outside of our comfort zones? We won't lie to you; sometimes you might find yourself a little out of your depth in Thailand. A lot of this is to do with the language barrier, which can often be prominent (unless you happen to be fluent in Thai... we're assuming you're not). You might feel a little uncomfortable at times, but if you remain calm, and keep smiling, you'll find a way through it, and you'll feel a stronger person for the experience.

Is it to do with experiencing a completely different culture? Unless you yourself are from East Asia, or you've traveled extensively there in the past, you won't be accustomed to being in a Buddhist country. Buddhism does strongly affect Thailand's culture, more than any other factor. This manifests itself in good ways though, even if it is different; it leads to politeness and respect in the vast majority of Thai people.

Is it to do with seeing some of the natural wonders of our amazing planet for the first time? The diversity of Thailand's landscape is simply incredible. You'll find coral reefs, tree-covered mountains, tall valleys, vast forests, waterfalls, plains, golden beaches, and much, much more, all in the same country. All this, of course, comes complete with a basically perfect holiday climate: always hot, and almost always sunny.

Is it to do with having completely new experiences? Well, how many times have you taken a kayak round a picture-perfect island to a secluded beach that was filled with monkeys? How many times have you walked through the ruins of a city that used to be the biggest on the planet? How many times have you hiked up a mountain to a giant, white Buddha statue, then gazed down at a broad valley full of twinkling lights? If it's new experiences you're after, you won't struggle to find them in Thailand.

Is it for a sense of freedom? In Thailand you'll find a culture which accepts foreigners regardless of size, sexuality or style. As long as you respect their culture, you can be whoever you want to be. The tourist infrastructure is also so excellent that you can construct any holiday you can dream of, to perfectly suit your needs. There are plenty of companies out there who will organize day trips or even your entire holiday. Alternatively, with an extensive and cheap transport system, you can quickly and easily go wherever you want, whenever you want. There are cheap restaurants and guesthouses for budget travelers, and fancy bistros and luxurious hotels for the more moneyed tourist.

We're guessing, as the kind of traveler who isn't content to simply explore their own country, or those nearby, that for you it's a mix of most or all of these. Whatever your traveling goals, Thailand ticks every single box for every single traveler.

There's a reason why Thailand can rely on tourism for a mighty 16% of its GDP. There's a reason why 30 million people visit annually, and why this number seems to rise every single year. There's a reason it's the second-most visited country in the enormous continent of Asia. Eventually, however un-alternative you are as a person, however much you hate to feel like a sheep, however many other people you know in your personal life who have already visited Thailand, you just have to follow the crowd. 30 million people every year can't be wrong.

Perhaps it's impossible to have a 'perfect' travel destination... but there aren't many countries out there which get closer than Thailand.

Made in the USA
Lexington, KY
21 April 2017